Intelligence
of the
Heart

A MEMOIR

SUSAN BELFIORE

Sail Away

ISBN (paperback): 9798218962432
ISBN (ebook): 9781088267325

Interior Design: Happenstance Type-O-Rama
Cover Design: Endpapers Studio

Sail Away

For Bill, your unconditional love has nurtured my soul, allowing me the fullest expression of myself.

And for Ramona, Loredana, Ionel, Mihaela, and Aidan— you all taught me what it means to love.

CONTENTS

Part I

Part II

Part III

FOREWORD

This poignant memoir tells the life story of a courageous woman who followed her heart from a comfortable existence in New Jersey to the chaos of a collapsing authoritarian regime during the last days of a Soviet Union satellite, where 120,000 abandoned children were being warehoused in hellish institutions as uninterested caregivers waited for them to die. In this unlikely environment, Susan Belfiore discovered four children who looked to her to find a better life. And she looked to them to provide the family for which she had long yearned.

Attempting to save those children and many others she encountered, Susan endured the nightmare of a sadistic game played by petty bureaucrats. Her mental and physical health strained, she was cursed, humiliated, lied to, laughed at, and ignored by officials who had no interest in caring for the children she had grown to love.

Susan gradually took the children out of the dark shadows of this human hellhole and brought them into the light. She has watched the four children who became her family grow into healthy and compassionate young people. This book shows the steps that Susan took to get here. It is a helpful guide to all who will read it, especially those who are attempting to follow their own hearts to do what is right in their lives.

> —Brother Toby McCarroll, a founding member
> of Starcross Community and the author of
> *Morning Glory Babies: Children with AIDS
> and the Celebration of Life* (St. Martin's Press)

INTRODUCTION

*The heart has its reasons
of which reason knows nothing.*

—BLAISE PASCAL,
philosopher and mathematician

We all have a story to tell; stories help us feel connected. I have two reasons why I have chosen to share my story. The first is straightforward. I have a friend who has encouraged me to share this story. After his many attempts over many years to persuade me, the simple words that finally convinced me were, "Susan, there is enough bad news out there; we need to hear something positive." These words felt right to me.

I started this book during the COVID pandemic, when the news was consistently bad, and fear was so thick it was hard to move. In fact, we weren't moving; we stopped traveling and stayed in our homes. In this atmosphere, I saw the need to acknowledge a time in my life that was life-affirming. A time when I opened up to new possibilities that I didn't even know existed.

My second reason for writing this book is more difficult to explain, but it speaks to a form of communication I feel is overlooked and yet powerful when acknowledged. I have come to realize that the decisions and unexpected learnings that have brought the most joy and growth in my life have come not from my mind, but, surprisingly, from my heart. The intelligence of my heart gave me a life I could not have imagined, a life I could never have planned for myself. This book speaks about times in my life when I allowed reason to take a back seat to my heart. I want to share this story to spotlight the power of the heart and its ability to guide us.

If I could manifest my greatest desire for this book, it would be that you might see a bit of yourself in these pages and that you will recognize or continue to recognize the power of your heart. You will identify and share your heart's story; we will open our communication from a place of love. We will gain comfort with the ways of the heart. Our lives will no longer be based solely on reason. It will be okay to not know why we know, to not question our heart-found, heart-led knowledge.

Part I

Prime Time: August 1990

It was a warm summer evening. The sound of the crickets could be heard from inside the kitchen. All the doors and windows were open to let a little heat of the day warm up the overly air-conditioned house. Someone, probably me, had forgotten to turn down the air before leaving that morning. Bill, my husband of twenty years, and I had lived in this very unusual postmodernist house for about three years, but I never got tired of how the fading sun played with the shadows on the wall. An associate of Michael Graves had designed it, and, like a home designed by Graves himself, it had many unusual angles and designs that caught the light.

Bill and I sat at the kitchen counter eating our dinner, a meal neither of us was very interested in. We were tired. Bill had a long commute home from New York City, where he worked on Wall Street. Traffic on Route 1 south to Princeton had been at its worst that night due to an accident. I didn't have a commute at all. I worked from an office in a separate building, only twenty feet away from the house. My work, called Hellerwork, entailed structural bodywork or myofascial manipulation and movement education. The work was physically demanding, and my weariness came from the sheer number of clients I had that day.

Although we were tired, we talked about our day and then moved on to the question of whether there was anything good to watch on TV. As we cleared our dishes, we decided to see if something might grab our attention. I curled up on the couch with our golden retriever, Falkor, at my feet. Because of problems with infertility, we didn't have any children; it looked like this big goofy dog that ate everyone's socks whole and leaped to kiss strangers was our heir apparent. Although it would have been nice to have children, we weren't unhappy. We had many friends and the support and love of our families, and most of all, we had each other.

Bill flipped through the stations looking for anything that would catch our interest.

"Wait a minute," I said, "Stop there!"

It was *Primetime Live* with Diane Sawyer. On the TV screen were babies, maybe twenty or twenty-five of them. The scene was shocking. Infants and toddlers with shaven heads, dressed in rags and rocking back and forth in their metal cribs. There were flies swarming around their heads and landing in their eyes. The children didn't even bother to swat them away. They were eerily quiet, with blank looks in their eyes. Some children looked ill; others were skin and bones. The room they were in was dark, and I saw nothing to stimulate them. I heard the announcer say that the children spent their whole lives in these cribs.

Then they showed an older gentleman, maybe in his sixties, with a white beard. He reminded me of Santa Claus. He was wearing black pants and a white shirt and had a plain wooden cross hung around his neck. I assumed that he was a clergyman.

A little boy with big, dark brown eyes raised his hands pleadingly for the clergyman to pick him up. The man seemed very upset as he lifted the small, dark-haired toddler from his crib.

I leaned in to hear what he was saying.

"This is intolerable. This has to stop. Something must be done," the clergyman said, while he walked around the room, observing and carrying the young boy with him.

When the man returned to the crib to put the dark-eyed little boy back down, the child wouldn't let go. I saw him cling tightly to the man's neck. As he peeled the child's hands from him, the clergyman uttered an emotional plea: "We have got to solve this problem!"

This scene broke my heart. I have never forgotten it, nor has its impact lessened with time.

The camera switched to Diane Sawyer, who identified the man as Brother Toby McCarroll, a member of Starcross, a Catholic community from Northern California. I learned that the children were Romanian. Romania had recently gone through a revolution, leaving the country with over one hundred thousand orphaned children. Ceaușescu, the country's despotic former president, had required families to have children they couldn't afford in order to build up the workforce. In addition to being orphaned, these children had been infected with the AIDS virus. Romania's failing health care system had unknowingly infected thousands of children through contaminated needles and commonly used blood transfusions. These innocent children had been abandoned and warehoused, left to die.

Brother Toby was an AIDS activist in the United States; he had come to Romania to assess the situation to see what could be done to help these children. The broadcast followed Brother Toby from Romania back to his home in California, to his own adopted family of five children, four of whom were infected with the AIDS virus. As their adoptive father, he now spoke live from California about a child's right to have a family, lead a normal life, and, when—or if—the time came, to not die alone. In 1990, children with AIDS were not expected to live more than five or six years. The contrast between the lives of children in Romania and his children was profound. The anchor explained that these children could not be brought into the US for help since there was a law here prohibiting anyone, even a child, from entering the country with HIV. This was 1990; the law had been in effect since 1987 and still had a majority of support in the Senate. This law reflected the fear and prejudice that surrounded AIDS in the US.

Diane Sawyer asked, "Brother Toby, do you still intend on helping the children in Romania?"

He responded, "Yes, very much so. But we can't do it alone."

"What do you need?" she asked.

"We need volunteers. Volunteers who are willing to put their own needs aside for a while. People who would be willing to come to Romania and stay at least six months, put up with a hard situation, be flexible, and most of all be willing to cry a lot."

As I watched and listened, I thought, *I'm really good at that last one.* Over the years, I had learned to appreciate a good cleansing cry; I no longer saw it as a weakness as I had in the past. The situation with the children in Romania was extremely sad; tears alone could not solve it, but Brother Toby seemed to realize that for someone to commit to helping these children, they could not be afraid to be moved deeply.

I believed that Brother Toby was speaking to me. Although I wasn't aware of it as I sat with Bill, watching the horror and heartbreak, this scene touched an unresolved part of my childhood. A part of my past I had walled up and packed deep down, so far down that I believed it had no effect on me. I felt proud when people would say, "You are so normal for having lost so much." Even though I had pride in my ability to carry on so well, I never spoke about my loss.

The scene playing across our television was the first shred of light to pierce through this wall in a long time. I thought to myself, *I could help these children,* not realizing that through them, I would be helping myself.

Bill and I were moved to tears, and as soon as the program ended, I quickly turned to him. "Do you think I should go?"

Without missing a beat, he said, "Yes."

We were on the same page, and it felt so good. This was an example of how our marriage had grown through the years. My heart filled with gratitude for this selfless man who now embodied, so effortlessly, a higher purpose for our marriage. This shared intention for our marriage led us to moments such as this, where we seemed to be of one mind.

The next day I got the details about Brother Toby's Starcross Community and sat down and wrote a letter. In the letter, I wrote about my work and personal background. The letter was not long, but the part that felt most important for me to say was this: *My belief in God does not allow me to believe that these children are victims. I cannot believe that these children were put on this earth solely to suffer and die. I believe that they were put here for a reason . . . to teach us. I feel like I am someone who could learn from them.*

I am not exactly sure why that was so important for me to say, but it was. Maybe because people with AIDS were being referred to as victims at that time. I didn't want to see these children as weak of spirit or somehow less than, marginalized because of a disease.

From that moment on, even before I sent the letter, Bill and I knew that I would be accepted by Starcross and sent to Romania.

Brother Tolbert McCarroll

"Brother Toby," as he is called by most who know him, is a man who has sought to live a contemplative life. This endeavor has often been challenged by his desire to help children in need.

In his former life, Brother Toby was an attorney for humanitarian causes. After raising his children and losing his wife, Brother Toby, along with Sisters Julie and Marti, founded Starcross Community, a small community in the monastic tradition. Their work together often led them to care for disadvantaged children in the US. Brother Toby has become the adoptive father of six children.

When I met Brother Toby, he had become an advocate for those who had been infected by HIV. Starcross Community had four children who carried the virus who were being fostered or adopted. His involvement with HIV/AIDS drastically increased after seeing a show on television about abandoned children who had AIDS living in subhuman conditions in Romania.

He traveled to Romania to see what could be done to help. He was so heartbroken by what he saw, he called for volunteers. I was one of them.

Childhood, 1950–1961

I was born June 2, 1950, to an Irish Catholic family from Long Island, New York. My father was a lawyer, and my mother was a homemaker. I have five siblings—three brothers and two sisters—and I am the youngest by far; my oldest brother was eighteen years older than me. I think my family thought of themselves as a typical middle-class family of the fifties. I'm not so sure that is correct, but keeping up appearances was important. I have a sense of this from what I've been able to gather from my early memories.

My brother-in-law told me that before he and my sister married, he was having dinner at our house, and my mother, an alcoholic, was upstairs threatening to kill herself as my father calmly said, "Please pass the butter." My father was known as a gentleman, so he would never have raised his voice or done anything that might have made a guest feel uncomfortable. Although I don't have any recollection of this time or other times I've learned about, I'm sure they added to my sense of uncertainty. Uncertainty, like my shadow, clung to me in those days.

Looking back on my early childhood, it feels fuzzy and unclear—a little like when I forget my reading glasses and try to read my texts on my phone. I can make out some words if I concentrate, but then other parts I just guess at, trying to decipher meaning from stray letters. That's how my childhood was, although instead of figuring it out in a timely manner, it has taken me years or decades to put the pieces together. This lack of clarity left me, in my early years, walking around in a fog.

My mother died the summer that I was six and she was fifty-one. That summer, our family had rented a beach house on the north fork of Long Island. The place was busy since four of my five siblings were there. My best friend, Shelly, was with me, so that made six kids and my parents. There were many hot summer days of swimming and warm nights sitting on the porch.

I have only three memories of that summer. One is my thirteen-year-old sister, Pat, getting in trouble and threatening to run away. It was very late, well after dark, when she returned, and I remember being afraid. I'm not sure if I was worried that she wouldn't come back or that she would and there would be more yelling. She was always getting in trouble, and I never got used to it. We roomed together when we weren't on vacation, so I had a front-row seat to all—the tears, yelling, and threats. On that night, the police were called. Thankfully, Pat walked through the door before they showed up.

My second memory is falling through the ceiling. My brother Mike slept in a dormer on the second floor. My parents were out shopping, and I'm pretty sure he was asked to watch me and wasn't happy about it. To keep me distracted so that he could read his comic book, Mike would have me close my eyes while he threw playing cards around his room. Then I had to find all fifty-two of them. One of the cards landed on an unfinished area of the dormer that was just beams and plasterboard. To retrieve the card, he told me to go carefully one foot and then two and then—I was through the ceiling. He watched me quickly disappear. I landed in the middle of the living room, surprising my parents, who were just coming in the door with packages. I got scrapes on my arms but was otherwise unscathed. To make me feel better, my parents gave me the new Davy Crockett drinking glasses they'd gotten at the gas station (as an incentive to buy gas), much to the disappointment of Rick, my ten-year-old brother.

My third memory is of my mother dying. I don't know much about it, even though I was there. She had a stroke late at night or early in the morning. My brother Rick came to my room, pulled down the shades, and told Shelly and me, "Something has happened. But I can't tell you what. You have to stay here."

Then the guessing game started as to what was going on.

I asked and then pleaded, "Is it good or bad?"

"Did something happen to Mom or Dad?"

"How about anyone else in the family?" Or maybe it was a surprise for us? It was kind of exciting to wake up to this game with my brother, who never wanted to play with us. I loved getting his attention. He was good at this game; no matter how we begged, he wasn't telling us.

Then I was sitting on the back stairs, the ones that went down to the kitchen. Here is where I can't see it clearly. Someone—maybe my twenty-four-year-old brother, Charlie—was telling me my mother had died.

That was it. She was gone . . . entirely and forever. No one ever spoke of her or asked me if I missed her. They never talked about what she cooked or liked to do. No one cried. I didn't go to a service or see her body go into the ground. She was just gone.

At the time, my mother's death didn't seem to bother anyone, so I guessed it wasn't supposed to bother me. I didn't have the chance to miss her around the house because I didn't go back to my home. I went to live with my twenty-something sister, Mary, who had three kids of her own. My father brought me there and told me I needed to stay because there was no one to care for me. I remember being really sad about not being able to go home with my dad. Not crying sad, but, like, in a fog sad; the world was even less clear. I loved my dad. He sang songs to me and would tell me stories that he made up. Every time I did him a favor (like getting his glasses), he would tell me I was a gentleman, a scholar, and a judge of good liquor. I heard these words so often that I never gave them much thought. It was only as I got older that I thought it was a strange thing to say to a six-year-old girl, but that was the Irish in him.

I loved my sister Mary, but living in her house was different from what I was used to. She was strict. I didn't know then, but later I learned that my mother had been a severe alcoholic, and as a result our home had had very little structure. I learned this fact from bits and pieces I overheard. When she was drinking, she gave little attention to raising us. She seemed to lie on the couch all day. Since I was so young, I'm not sure how accurate that recollection is, but when I picture my mother in my mind, the only image I have is of her lying on the couch. A neighborhood friend told me that if it weren't for her developmentally delayed daughter, who often watched me, I would have gotten hurt or fallen down the stairs. This explained why my sister's home felt so hard for me. I had chores, bedtime, and cleanup to do; I felt like Cinderella. I was in first grade and my second school while I lived with Mary; my father would visit on weekends when he could.

My father got remarried in the spring of that year, eight months after my mother's death. He married a widow, also named Mary, whom he had known for many years. They hadn't seen each other in a very long time, but he sat next to her at my cousin's wedding, and they decided to marry soon after. To complicate matters, Mary had been married to my second cousin by marriage, and now she was my stepmother. Mary also had five children, making my cousins once removed now my stepsiblings. I love to tell this story when I want to confuse someone, especially after drinking. My stepmother often told me that when my father proposed to her, he didn't say, "Mary, I love you." Instead, he said, "Mary, I need you."

We (four of us kids, and one of her five) all moved into a house together in Manhasset, Long Island. I started the second grade and my third school in three years. I was sick frequently with unexplained fevers. I spent a week in the hospital with the doctors trying to diagnose me until my stepmother decided it was "just" nerves. Today, it would be called anxiety. Since I had missed a lot of school, I arrived at my new school, St. Mary's, feeling way behind the other kids. My father thought that Catholic education was the best, so we all went to parochial schools. I don't know how the best education was supposed to work with sixty girls in my classroom and one teacher. I do know it didn't work for me. I had missed the lessons on sounding out letters and words, and reading wasn't making sense to me. I started to dislike school because I wasn't feeling successful and because I feared the nuns. By the time I got to third grade, I was so far behind I needed to repeat the year. Instead of recognizing my situation as the result of circumstances beyond my control, I saw myself as a failure, a feeling that stayed with me for many years. It wasn't until I was in my late teens, when I had a clearer perspective of my early years, that this feeling started to diminish.

St. Mary's had one thing going for it. It was where I was going to make my first communion, and that was special. I remember feeling so saint-like and holy on

17

that day. I wore a white dress trimmed with lace, white patent leather shoes, and a veil. I approached the altar with great anticipation, wondering how I would feel after receiving Jesus's body in mine. When the time came, I thought I did feel a little different, but when my dad gave me such a loving look and called me his angel, I knew I was not the same; I *felt* like an angel.

The three of us—my dad, my new mom, and I—went out for breakfast. I had never recalled being alone with my parents before. I had no brothers or sisters competing for their attention; they were all mine. It was a day I knew I would never forget.

A part of my life that I would still like to understand more clearly is my relationship with the Catholic Church and how it has affected my life. I know as a child, I believed all that I was taught. I feared doing wrong because I believed in retribution. I was also comforted by God when I was afraid. I prayed each night for my family and felt connected with God when I went to church. I know there's more to say about the church and how it affected my life, but these simple things helped me with what happened next.

About two years after my mother died, my father died. I was eight years old. It had been only a year and a half since he had married Mary, my stepmother. This time it was my stepmother who told me about his death. He'd had a heart attack when he came home from work two nights before. I was sent to the neighbor's house. The ambulance was told not to use their sirens so as not to scare me. But I saw the ambulance lights on the wall of the neighbor's home, and I was scared; my legs trembled and my heart beat fast.

The next day I was brought to my best friend's house, the same girl who had been with me when my mother died. We were playing on the floor of her room with our play horses, and I got called downstairs to see my stepmother. She put her arm around me and told me that my father had gone to live with my mother in heaven. I don't remember anything else she said or if I cried. If I did, it was very little. After a bit, she said I could stay and go back up and play. As I entered Shelly's room, she told me she was sorry. I said thanks, and we went back to playing. After some time, I remember thinking, *How strange that my father died and I'm still playing.*

Life changed drastically after my father's death. I had just been getting used to the setup with my new mother. I might have even liked some of her new ways; children did the dishes and I had to set the table, clean my room, and make my bed. I liked that each week she would buy flowers at the market to have in the house. She knew how to make a home. The only part I didn't like was cocktail time each night with my dad. She made that time off-limits to the kids—just her and my dad. So there was no longer any sitting on his lap, getting all of his attention, when he came home from work. I didn't like this one bit, but even that, I'd been getting used to. Things were becoming predictable for the first time.

After his death, my stepmother gave me a choice to stay with her or to go back and live with my sister

Mary. My brother Rick, four years older, and I wanted to stay together, and I wanted a mother of my own, so we chose to stay with my stepmother. My older brother Mike went to live with my oldest brother Charlie, and my sister Pat, the one who was always in trouble, went to live with my sister Mary.

My stepmother, who I now referred to as my mother, owned a liquor store and a home in Huntington, Long Island. These assets were from her first marriage, and it was a good thing that she had them since she told me later in life that my father had had many bills when he died. In fact, soon after his death, his car was repossessed. Even though my father had been an attorney and had a decent income, he hadn't managed his money well.

I was now living in Huntington, my fourth move and another new school. The fog I was in deepened; I was in shock. In school, I wasn't successful. When we would line up and walk down the hallway, I would play a game with myself. If I could keep my shoes inside the tiles and not step on a crack, I would know the answers when we returned to class.

I was tall. Out of the sixty girls, I was the second tallest. I didn't like my height at all. The small girls looked so nice in their uniforms that fit just right. My pea-green uniform made me look like the Green Giant. The small girls all had black patent leather shoes; I had brown oxfords. My mother was sensible, she said. I wanted to be as cute as the little girls; I felt gawky. Not many of the cute girls spoke to me. The small girls sat up front; the tall ones were in the back. But when we did speak, I felt so awkward because I needed to bend over to hear them. In an attempt to help me look better, my mother gave me a home permanent. When she took the curlers out, I could tell it wasn't good because she was already speaking about how we could wash it out. My hair was awful. It was curly, frizzy, and tight to my head, and it didn't wash out. I now saw myself as an overly tall, thin, blonde-haired girl with this curly, frizzy mess on my head. I felt like I stood out like a sky dancer in front of a gas station.

Aside from school, I wasn't feeling that unhappy. I had two neighborhood friends that I played with after school. My brother, my mother, and I were a small but happy enough family, though I didn't see my birth family very much and missed them. Since I was with my stepmother, I was more involved with my stepsiblings. If I complained to my mother that I hadn't heard from my siblings, she would tell me not to feel sorry for myself and if I wanted to speak with them, I should call them. I don't know how much I did that at ten years old.

On the other hand, my brother Rick was really unhappy and missed our family. When he was thirteen, he took the initiative to go visit our sister Mary. She lived about forty-five minutes away with her husband and four children. One day when my mother was at work, Rick stuck out his thumb on our busy road. When the first car that stopped offered us a ride, he told me to jump in. I questioned this idea for a brief moment and then got in. In the front were a very nice

"Ozzie and Harriet" sort of couple. They asked me how old I was and my name. They said they had kids but didn't like the thought of them hitching. They said they thought it was better that they take us instead of who knows what. I was happy they took us most of the way. We walked the last bit, thinking about how happy and surprised Mary would be to see us.

Mary was anything but happy; she was angry as a hornet. I can still see the confusion on her face as she opened the door.

"What are you doing here?" she asked, not giving us time to answer. "How did you get here? You what? With your sister?" she screamed at Rick.

We were driven back home and told to promise never to do that again. That was the last attempt we made to see our family until we were much older.

In my eleventh year, my mother moved her liquor store business about an hour east to Babylon. This is where the most enduring person in my life was waiting, unbeknownst to him and me.

Starcross, 1991

The muddy path I follow
Points up the hill
Near the top and off to the side
Stands an old apple tree
Sitting on a weather dish
Is a golden child
Clapping her hands as the
Apple blossoms fall

—Brother Tolbert McCarroll

It wasn't long until I heard that I was officially accepted into the training program at Starcross. I was notified in the middle of September and was to arrive at the training program in California on October 31. My commitment to Starcross was six months, until the end of April. I was to train for two months in California and then spend four months in Romania, helping with the overwhelming number of abandoned and HIV-infected children.

Starcross Community is located in northwestern Sonoma County in Annapolis, California, about two hours north of San Francisco. It is a magnificent area with rolling hills, acres and acres of vineyards, and awe-inspiring giant redwoods. It is a little bit of heaven on earth. But getting to this area can test your resolve as to whether you really want to go to heaven.

There are two ways to get there. One is the nail-biting Pacific Coast Highway (State Route 1), with turns around steep cliffs that make you feel like the ocean is your next stop. The other is a drive of miles and miles on extremely winding roads, with hairpin turns that can have those with the strongest of stomachs turning green.

Starcross is located on a Christmas tree farm. It is the home of the Starcross monastic community members, Brother Toby, Sister Julie, Sister Marti, and their adopted and foster children. The community had always considered themselves a contemplative group, a practice that would be difficult to maintain once they added the commitment of helping Romania's children.

The barn on the property was situated close to the road on the left side of a long driveway. The barn had a cow and room to make and package Christmas wreaths and trees. Across from the barn was an old farmhouse with a bustling kitchen. For the two months that I was in training before going to Romania, I spent time both at the Starcross farm and its satellite city location in Santa Rosa.

I was one of six volunteers who had come to train with Brother Toby and his two right hands, Sister Julie and Sister Marti. There were also volunteers who helped with the Starcross children or worked on the farm and helped with packaging wreaths and trees. In both places, there were many people to feed and care for.

We were there to learn about Romania, HIV/AIDS, and child care. In addition to preparing to go to Romania, we were to help around the farm since it was the time leading up to Christmas, their busiest season.

The Romanian volunteers stayed in a trailer-like building on the same side of the driveway as the barn; Brother Toby lived in a similar structure nearby. When standing at any location on the farm, no matter which way you looked, you could take in the beauty of the land. To the south, you saw row upon row of pine trees; to the north, giant redwoods; to the east, rolling hills; and to the west, meadows whose color changed with the time of day and season. Up the hill from the bustle of the farm is a small chapel with big windows. The building might hold fifty people at most, but I can't imagine that there would ever be the want for more than that. The beauty and spiritual nature of the place comes from the solitude that it offers. The serene feeling that overcomes you when you enter is so welcoming that you might want to bathe in it long past your allotted time. Looking out and down across the fields, seeing the shadows of the sun, the antics of the squirrels and birds, and other gifts of nature, you might feel that instead of saying a prayer, you are *in* a prayer.

Having arrived just a few days earlier, I was still learning the secrets of the land. As I walked the property, my thoughts turned to when I said good-bye to Bill at the airport, the last hug before I boarded the plane. I looked at him and said, in a shaky, teary voice, "What am I doing? I don't know these people at Starcross. I hardly know anything about Romania and little to nothing about HIV/ AIDS. What am I doing, leaving you and committing to this project for the next six months?"

He looked at me in a way I know all so well, a look of, "You can do it, Susan." So, with that silent encouragement, I believed I could and got on the plane.

When I arrived in California, I had to figure out which bus to catch to Santa Rosa, about forty-five minutes away, where Starcross had another home. Morning Glory House was so named because, just as the flower blooms early in the morning, children with AIDS bloom early in life. Santa Rosa is where Starcross residents do their shopping, send their children to school, meet with friends, and attend to any financial business. Morning Glory House is a nice enough four-bedroom home but does not lend itself to contemplation the way the farm does. The community spends as much time as they can at the farm, so they travel back and forth between the city and the farm a couple of times a week. This was true for us as volunteers also; we went where we were needed.

When I arrived in Santa Rosa, I was greeted at the bus by another volunteer, Stephanie, a twenty-eight-year-old preschool teacher from New Mexico. She had been there for three weeks or so and tried to fill me in, but in my nervousness, I couldn't take in what she had to say. If I had, I wouldn't have been surprised by the greeting I got when I arrived at the house.

The greeting was a chilly one. I was surprised to find out the community consisted of just three people: Brother Toby, Sister Marti, and Sister Julie. They were sitting down to lunch when I arrived. There was no one coming out to greet me with hugs and appreciation for coming to help.

Instead, Sister Marti said in a soft, rushed voice, "Put your things down; we will be with you in a while. If you are hungry, go into the kitchen and get some lunch; Margaret will help you. After that, you can put your things upstairs. Stephanie will show you where."

Then she was off. I don't know what I had expected, but this was not it. The days and weeks before I left home, I had been feeling pretty special, receiving calls of admiration for my willingness to help in Romania, a going-away party, and a blessing way from my girl-friends (a women's ritual of acknowledging and sup-porting major changes in each other's lives). Now there was nothing special about me.

I was standing in the midst of a bustling home of many children, adults, and a cat and dog, all with directed activity, not knowing where I fit in. I wished I had listened to Stephanie a little better and maybe read between the lines. I might have picked up that the three people who made up Starcross had taken on a massive project on top of their already demanding lives of taking care of five children under age five, two homes, a Christmas tree farm, and a business crafting and selling wreaths. It was November 1, the very beginning of their seasonal business. Their primary source of income selling Christmas wreaths and trees was just starting up, and now they had volunteers for Romania arriving.

"It was not the best or even a good time to take on such a project, but we had no choice," I heard Sister Marti say over the phone one day. "The children of Romania were living and dying like caged animals. They can't wait. They need help now."

As if all this weren't enough, Tina, Sister Julie's adopted daughter and a child of Starcross, was extremely ill with complications from the AIDS virus. One of the first things I learned from the volunteers was that Tina's half-birthday party was being planned for that week; the implication of this wasn't hard to understand.

In the next two days, I was introduced to all the volunteers who were, like me, going to Romania. My first impressions were that Stephanie was fun and a little mysterious. Sarah, a forty-year-old mother of two boys from Connecticut, seemed straightforward and bossy, and Chuck, a thirty-three-year-old land surveyor from Alabama with a strong Southern accent, seemed easygoing. I can't recall much about the other two volunteers in our group, Mary and Carol, since they left the program after only a short time. Either they decided for themselves, or the Starcross members decided for them, that they weren't a good fit for the program. We were from all across the United States. After meeting everyone, I began to wonder about the selection process. I don't know about the others, but I wondered why I was chosen; I had heard that there were hundreds of inquiries. Why me? The answer to that question wasn't evident to me then, nor is it today.

I met all the children of Starcross out at the swing set, where they got busy checking me out. I was glad they seemed as interested in me as I was in them.

Niki was the oldest, at five years old, with dark brown hair. Then came David, age four, the only boy and the only child not infected with the virus. Michele, age three, was all action, and then there was two-and-a-half-year-old Tina and the baby, Holly.

Tina had been overtaken with the AIDS virus, and at that time, there were few drugs to help her condition. Sister Julie and Starcross tried, but there was little anyone could do for her. Although Tina's body would not be able to fight off the disease, her strong spirit affected many people's lives, including mine.

After a few days, I was getting the hang of the training and beginning to know and like the other volunteers. But I felt awkward with the community members. They seemed to be overwhelmed. We had a long lecture from Brother Toby about the conditions we would be facing in Romania, and it all sounded worse than I had been expecting.

From behind his massive desk, loaded with piles of papers, Brother Toby announced, "I want you to know clean air, clean water, food, and heat are hard to come by. The conditions with the government are getting worse." But, he added, "Everything is changing quickly." *Oh great*, I thought as I looked around at a group of blank faces. If my fellow volunteers were having a problem with this, they weren't showing it.

Our days were packed full; we learned about Romania, its politics, and the child care system. We also learned how the state was dealing with HIV/AIDS. Sister Julie gave us talks on the Starcross philosophy of child care. "When caring for a child," she explained, "you never withhold love or food when disciplining. Also, we might need to schedule our time so that each child gets held for at least an hour every day."

We had medical personnel teach us about HIV and how to protect ourselves and others. They also gave us a basic explanation of how the virus works. Brother Toby was responsible for providing us with our fundamental knowledge of Romania.

When we were not in a seminar, we were either caring for the children, helping in the kitchen, or helping with wreaths and trees. I loved being with the children but wasn't thrilled about packing the wreaths. But I had said that I could be flexible, so I kept my thoughts to myself.

Most days were physically tiring, but some were harder emotionally. I remember one day feeling so judged by Sister Marti. I knew that if I was feeling judged, I must be doing the same to her. We both had decisions to make: Marti was trying to decide if I was suitable for the project, and I was deciding whether this organization was right for me.

But something else was there, something that was bothering me that wasn't as clear, making me feel uneasy. I didn't feel appreciated for who I was. This went deeper than whether I was right for the program. It was more at a soul level. I remembered that through my upbringing at home and through the church, I had to prove myself to be accepted. I was taught that I wouldn't be allowed into heaven to experience all of God's glory unless I lived a certain way of life. This was in opposition to my beliefs for the last couple of decades.

I had been through a long search to find my place with God. Initially, as a child, I believed all that the church told me; after that, I questioned all of it. As a Unitarian in my twenties, when asked to stand on a continuum as an awareness exercise—with strong belief in God on one end and no belief in God on the other—I stood on the farthest end, away from acknowledging God. I didn't even want to hear his/her name. Now, in my forties, I had found a way of connecting to a force so strong that it didn't matter what it was called. It was no longer a concept; it was an experience. I had learned through my work, books, and spiritual teachers of unconditional love and the power of the heart.

Now at Starcross, I felt myself contracting, pulling back, a feeling I hadn't had since I was young. A presence there reminded me of my Catholic upbringing, a sense of never being enough, born in sin. When I was younger, I had felt that I was deemed wrong and needed to prove myself worthy. This attitude was old and had taken me so long to overcome. I wasn't sure exactly what had triggered that feeling. I hoped that I could maintain my sense of self and stay open to the community.

In early December, Dr. Matusa, an infectious disease specialist, arrived from the port city of Constanta, Romania, where it is believed that sailors brought the virus to shore. There, she was in charge of over a thousand HIV-positive children, more than the total number of infected children in the US. She was to observe the lifestyle of the Starcross children and to learn about the latest medical treatments in the US for HIV/AIDS. At Brother Toby's request, Dr. Matusa spent her time at both the local hospital and Starcross.

A short-statured, quietly powerful woman in her fifties, Dr. Matusa seemed to be able to stay sensitive and compassionate amid a disproportionate amount of sickness and death. Sarah was charged with caring for Dr. Matusa, and I had just a few moments with her. I longed to ask her many questions about life in Romania and the state of the children who would be in our care. But it was becoming clear that Dr. Matusa had her own adjusting to do.

At lunch, Sarah said, "Dr. Matusa got lost in the supermarket today. When I found her, she was in front of the bananas, crying."

"There is so much of everything here," Dr. Matusa had said through her tears. "I haven't seen a banana in almost twenty years."

Sarah told me later that Dr. Matusa also said that the cost of the plane ticket was equivalent to three months of her salary.

Brother Toby told us he wanted us to move into one of the *post curas* (meaning "after the hospital," these are the residential quarters where the children live after they leave the hospital) in Constanta, about 225 kilometers from Bucharest. We soon learned from Dr. Matusa that this building had no heat or hot water. She would be attending to the children's medical needs, plus so many more of our needs yet to be established.

Then Brother Toby told us flatly, "You each will be given five children to care for." Initially, five children didn't seem so bad. My sisters had raised five and six kids. It sounded doable.

Then I thought about it more: five children at once, all under three, with no heat or hot water, and food hard to come by. This plan sounded like a challenge. I needed to trust that between Brother Toby and Dr. Matusa, they knew what was possible. For me, it would take a leap of faith.

One day we gathered around the small farmhouse table, where everyone had been asked to meet for lunch, as Brother Toby filled us in on the horrid conditions of life in Romania. There was a lull in the conversation, and I decided to speak up about what was on my mind.

Looking directly at Brother Toby, I said, "I understand that our whole purpose in going to Romania is to care for the children. I get that. But I have no sense of how you will support us while we're there." I paused and looked around the table to see if my fellow volunteers were feeling similarly. Instead, they were looking down at their plates. I continued, "I mean, how can you ensure our safety over there? It seems dangerous."

By now, my voice was getting a little shaky since I wasn't getting an immediate response from anyone. I was unsure if my colleagues agreed with me or if I was a lone wolf. I had voiced my thoughts with the other volunteers, and I thought they shared my concern. But where were they now? At that moment, I didn't believe Brother Toby was upset with me, but I'm not sure he answered my question either. Whatever he said, he didn't answer it directly. I decided to put my question aside to see if my concerns would be addressed in time. I didn't want Toby and the sisters to feel criticized, but I was beginning to feel that the situation in Romania was indeed dangerous.

My favorite assignment at this halfway mark in the training was my time with Tina. Tina was born in Hawaii; her mother had been infected with the virus, couldn't care for her, and gave her up for adoption. Sister Julie received Tina as an infant. In the past six months, her immune system had started to fail. As a result, outwardly, she suffered from chicken pox sores on her arms and mouth and ran fevers. Inside, the virus was breaking down her system and taking over. I spent a couple of nights with Tina to allow Julie to get some sleep. I spent much of the night rocking, singing to her, telling her stories, or doing whatever I could to distract her from her pain.

She was a very definite little one. She would wave you off if she wasn't in the mood for you. So far, I hadn't been waved off, which was great because I loved my time with her. It was after one of these nights with her that I wrote this poem:

To Tina
So small
You look at me with the wisdom of a
Thousand years
A body so frail
How have you learned to withstand
The pain of what we do not know?
Each moment I am with you
Your aliveness and your death walk
Hand and hand

The day after I wrote this poem, ABC's *Primetime Live* crew arrived at Starcross to film a follow-up piece on the Romanian project. They interviewed me and asked me to read my poem about Tina. I spoke with Julie about their request. As I read my poem to her, she started to cry.

I immediately felt terrible. Who was I to speak about her child dying? What did I know? We both cried. I felt very close to her at that time; I still do. She spoke about how hard it was and how she wished that she could give her body to Tina. This was a love that I don't think I knew of—to give my life for another. I felt so vulnerable and unsure of myself.

She said, "You should read it, but leave out the part about death." She continued, "I think of it often, but I don't speak of it."

So I read the poem and other entries from my journal, but I left out the part about death. I didn't feel that what I had to contribute to the TV filming mattered much, but Tina mattered, and I felt compelled to speak about her.

From Brother Toby, we finally heard about the specifics of our project. We would be taking over one of the post curas, where the children lived in steel cribs. The hospital wards would be transformed into small apartments, each of which would become the "home" for five children, with one mother or caretaker per family. The intention was that the children get out of their beds, lead normal lives, and bond with each other and their caretaker. This was the Starcross model. By doing this, we hoped that the children's health would improve. And if the virus were to overcome them, no child would have to die alone again.

Brother Toby told us what each of our positions would be. Chuck was put in charge of our living environment (water, heat, housing, etc.). Stephanie became cellarer, in charge of community supplies. Sarah was named Coordinator of Operations. I was told I'd be a chaplain, or the person in charge of the children's spiritual welfare. I didn't yet have an exact title, but I felt honored and happy to be in charge of this area.

It was now the middle of December, and each day was like a roller coaster with the highs of celebrating the season, the lows of the virus, and Tina's fight for her life. Moreover, we experienced the high of getting closer to helping the children in Romania and the lows of the constant obstacles to overcome.

One day, we celebrated with the children by singing Christmas carols, baking cookies, reading Christmas stories, and decorating the house. That night Tina, in pain, had to be taken to the hospital. There was a new medication available. We prayed that it would work. Her next day at the hospital, she felt much better, not yet from the medication, but that's just how the virus works: up one day, down the next. I remember looking at her, sleeping so peacefully in her bed with her slightly flushed cheeks and wispy hair, as the little girl in the next room was screeching in pain and fear. Such a contrast. I felt gratitude looking at this sleeping child, knowing how quickly her condition could change.

We were getting closer to our Romanian departure date. Brother Toby had secured a building for us. I was in awe of his ability to handle all of this with little and poor communication equipment in Romania. Much of the communication happened by fax. The phone was slow, and the connection was unreliable.

As the volunteers gathered around the country kitchen table one day, we shared our excitement and travel plans. Out of nowhere, Brother Toby entered to tell us there was a change in plans. Richard, who I had only heard of, was coming home. I didn't know precisely what that meant, but it didn't sound good coming from Toby's mouth. Sarah and Chuck would now be leaving earlier for Romania, on December 27. He went on to say, "Conditions in Romania are not good—a travel advisory has been posted. There are demonstrations and protests in the streets." Toby exited as quickly as he'd arrived, ending with, "But nothing will stop us!" That made me nervous.

We continued our emotional roller coaster down a steep decline when Tina came home from the hospital. She had a difficult morning. She had not had any Benadryl since 12:30 a.m. There was a time when Julie and I were with her that her pain was so raw, it was almost unbearable. It was good to have her home, but her pain overshadowed the joy. What if this medicine didn't work? I had to believe it would.

As Christmas approached, the festivities of the season increased, and the wreath and tree work of the farm settled down. Brother Toby seemed to become more alive with all the rituals of this time of year. He was actively involved with the children as they continued to prepare for the holiday. Romania had kept him so busy, but he was now enjoying his extra time as another gift of the season. David on violin, Sister Marti on cello, and Sister Julie on piano performed a concert for Brother Toby and the volunteers, followed by some Christmas carols. Any feelings I'd had of not feeling connected with the community were gone.

I planned to go to my brother Rick's house in Utah for the holiday. It had been twenty years since I had been with him for Christmas. Bill would be there by the time I arrived. Although I'd recently been with him at Thanksgiving, the thought that I would be in Romania soon magnified my need to see him.

Before I left for the holiday, I heard Julie and Tina had gone back to the farm; thankfully, Tina was having some good days. This news added to my Christmas spirit.

I was alone at Morning Glory House, having had a teary phone conversation with a friend about how much I missed home. I heard a knock at the door. It was the woman from the drug rehab house across the street. She was young, in her early twenties, dressed in a tracksuit. She shyly gave me an envelope containing twenty-six dollars and change. The envelope read, "Please give what you can to help children with AIDS." As she handed me the envelope, she said, "Please use this money to help with the children in Romania." It was so moving that this woman and others who were struggling themselves cared enough to raise money for Romania's children. Merry Christmas, indeed.

Christmas at my brother's house did not disappoint: it was all that I thought it would be and more. The only problem was I wasn't feeling well. I had picked up a really bad cold when I was with Tina in the hospital. Bill, of course, was the best medicine for me. He was so warm and caring. Laughing with him hurt my ribs but healed my soul.

On Christmas evening, Bill and I spoke about going to Romania. I'd started to feel nervous after our last report from Brother Toby. Bill got me in touch with what the trip would be about and how I had a chance to make a difference. I wondered if he was really so steadfast or just acting that way in front of me.

Before I knew it, I was back at Starcross for our final days of training. I learned that Tina had gone back to the hospital before Christmas. The new medication was not working. Brother Toby said that she could have two weeks or nine months. They were now giving her medication containing opium for the pain.

When I started this training, I realized that I had been cavalier about these children and death. My attitude was that I could handle it. I thought I knew of death. But I didn't, really. I never knew until then that death and hope walk hand in hand. That, when needed, our job for our children would be to hold hope as strongly as death might be calling. From Tina, I learned that hope showed its face many times a day. The name of our home in Romania would be Casa Speranta (House of Hope). The name had now taken on a new, deeper meaning for me.

* * *

On one of our last nights of training, Stephanie and I took a late-night walk around Santa Rosa. Although it was January, it was a warm, misty evening. Before our walk, Brother Toby had held a special blessing for our departure and mission. Brother Toby, Sister Marti, Sister Julie, Stephanie, and I attended.

Brother Toby said, "This time, I feel so different than my last trip. On my last trip, I felt so incomplete; I felt that I hadn't done anything to help the children.... Now I'm going back and bringing you to stay longer; I feel like something is happening."

He looked at us and added, "I know that none of you is perfect to do what we need to do. Yet it is your passion that will fill the gaps."

He spoke beautifully but only of his experience. He didn't inquire about anyone else or their experience. This had always confused me about him. I sensed that it wasn't that he didn't care, but that he assumed he already knew how we thought and felt.

To fill the gap left by our lack of sharing, on our walk Stephanie and I shared our experiences and insights. We stopped along the way to appreciate the abundance of goods in the stores, a sight we thought we might not see for a while.

My last night at Starcross was very emotional; saying goodbye to Julie and Tina was hard. Julie was in so much pain. She tearfully said, "Tina isn't doing well at all, Susan." Her comment surprised me; it was so apparent.

She continued to say, "Please tell the people in Romania, at Casa Speranta, about Tina and what she's like."

I quickly told her, "That won't be a problem. She's meant so much to me." In the morning, Julie left their pictures in an envelope attached to my door. My heart sank as I wondered if I would ever see them again. I felt so connected with Julie. We both tried to overcome our differences to be together, knowing that we wouldn't be together long. I didn't know what our relationship had been about, but I knew it had been special. I felt honored to have had Julie and Tina in my life.

Letting Go of
Poor Susan, 1960s

My stepmother's business became successful. It seems she had a head for business. For the first time in her life, she had some extra money to spend. Her financial success allowed her to travel and buy a home on the water in Babylon, a midsize town on the south shore of Long Island.

The day Bill and I met, we were with our mothers in a big department store similar to today's Walmart. The year was 1962, and we were both twelve years old. My dad had died four years before, and my birth mother two years prior to that; my memories of them felt like they were fading. When I saw this redheaded boy with freckles, I thought I recognized him from school. I knew our brothers were friends; I had heard my brother talk about how good he was at basketball. We barely and shyly said hi to each other, but something unspoken happened. Neither of us can remember what caused us to feel so connected from that small encounter, but from that day forward, we considered each other to be boyfriend and girlfriend.

Bill says that for him, it was my long blonde hair that attracted him. I just thought he was cute. I started to write his name on my books. He would call me right after school. Since there wasn't much dating to do at that age, we would attend basketball games together. Bill's brother was an all-star player, so his father would pick me up, and we would all go together. Our first sort of date was a roller skating party. We ended up holding hands awkwardly as we went around and around the rink. What started off as exciting ended up just being uncomfortable, with sweaty hands that didn't know how to let go. But later that week, Bill invited me to a party at his house in the finished basement. The Beatles had just put their first record out. I sat close to him as "I Want to Hold Your Hand" played on the record player.

Bill also lived in Babylon with his family in a development about two miles closer to town than I did. The Twin Oaks homes were built in the early fifties and looked very similar to each other. These affordable houses attracted young couples who wanted to move out of the cities to the suburbs to raise their kids. Although Bill would often say he came from the other side of the tracks, referring to my slightly bigger home (we had two bathrooms, he had one), we were on the same side. In his neighborhood, you could hear the sound of children playing. It was a strong community where the adults watched out for each other's children, ran contests for the best Christmas decorations, and talked over the fence with their neighbors. My neighborhood had mostly older couples (my mother was sixty-five) and was more sedate than Bill's. But I loved our house. It had a beautiful view overlooking the Great South Bay, where I would fish, swim, clam, sail, water ski, and do anything else that had to do with the water.

As we moved from our preteens into our teens, our relationship continued. Bill was very athletic, and I attended all of his games. He was on the football team, basketball team, and lacrosse team. If the game included a ball, he was very confident that he would excel at it. I liked that about him, but most of all, I liked that he made me laugh like no one else could. He had a way of saying shocking things that might be on everyone's minds but they would never say. He was irreverent, a kind of humor that I have appreciated from the time I met him. Of course, it rubbed some adults the wrong way, especially my mother, who felt children should be seen but not heard. Many times, she would say, "That Billy Belfiore is a fresh kid." Their relationship was never good, but as the years went by, they learned to tolerate each other.

I was finally feeling settled in our new home. I was the happiest I had ever felt. School was easier than in the past; I was now in a public school. There were thirty students in my class instead of sixty, making the whole atmosphere more relaxed. I was no longer a frizzy-headed giant. My hair was long and blonde, and I felt like I fit in since the other girls in my class were now closer to my height. I seemed to make friends effortlessly, although I was still bashful.

Summer was my favorite time of year. Since we lived on the water and there was a yacht club behind my house, my mother gave me swimming and sailing lessons. I can still feel the warmth of those summer days. I would wake up early as my mother was leaving for work. She would give me a list of chores for the day. Dressed in my cut-off jeans, with my hair pulled back in a ponytail and bare feet, I would complete my list and then head to the club for the day. There I would meet up with a friend to swim or sail. We would swim for hours or race our boats. We might also water ski, clam, crab, or fish. But my absolute favorite thing to do was to sail way out toward the bridge. The bridge was visible from our house but miles away. I always brought a friend because that was my mother's rule. But despite needing to have someone with me, I had such a sense of freedom the farther I got from shore. I loved feeling the warmth of the sun and playing with the wind. I always felt so accomplished when I returned to shore, realizing I had maneuvered through whatever the wind and water handed me: heavy gusts, no wind, a strong current, or rough waves. I would turn around and look toward the bridge, knowing I had conquered that distance.

But, the older I got, the harder life at home with my mother became. My older brother, Rick, who by this time wasn't getting along with her, had been sent to boarding school and soon after joined the US Air Force. Now I began running into problems with her. She had little or no patience for teenagers or anyone who didn't agree with her. She didn't have the capacity to listen to another point of view or to negotiate. As a result, we seemed to fight about everything. She didn't believe that children should have or were worthy of an opinion. The more I formed opinions and eagerly shared them with her, the harder it was for us to be together.

I remember so well sitting with her and a friend or two of hers in the living room or in the summer on the patio for cocktail hour. I was encouraged to be there but not to say anything aside from some initial pleasantries. I'm not sure why she wanted me at her evening ritual, but I was both amazed and bored to death by her desire to dominate the conversation. If her friend interjected, it would be only minutes until my mother brought the conversation back around to herself. This informal training taught me to be a good listener, or at least look like one, and it just about took my voice away. If I did take a chance and express my opinion, I was met with ridicule.

Sometimes, especially after a drink or two, she could get a mean edge to her, as when she turned to me one Easter dinner, when we weren't getting along, and asked, in front of my older stepbrothers and sisters, "Susan, do you know what sixty-nine means?"

My petite, gray-haired, seventy-something-year-old stepmother was asking me, a fifteen-year-old, this at the dinner table.

Wanting to be seen as mature in front of my older stepsiblings, I said yes. This was a big mistake. Now she wanted me to tell everyone what it meant; she was demanding it. I was mortified until one of my stepsisters stepped in and changed the subject.

It wasn't just me my mother ridiculed. I saw my Aunt Eileen and other friends of hers put up with it for years until one day, they each told my mother "enough," and she never saw them again.

I don't hold her totally responsible for our problems; after all, I was a teenager who had some issues to deal with. At times she really tried, like by buying me a sailboat and a piano—things to make me feel good about myself. Also, during the summer I turned sixteen, she adopted me. She told me that she wanted me to feel that I belonged. But not much changed afterward; we still couldn't get along. I had such conflicting feelings toward her. I was grateful that she cared for me after my parents died. Where would I have gone otherwise? She didn't have to take me in—at fifty-five, she didn't need an eight-year-old. But when I would tell her I loved her, she would respond with, "The feeling is likewise, dear." Her Irish Catholic upbringing was early 1900s, with a strict father and an emotionally distant mother, and didn't allow for any more expression than that. And that's what I longed for from her.

Her way of dealing with conflict was to stop talking to me, sometimes for a week or more. It was during one of these silent periods that I found out she was retiring from her business and moving in with my stepsister, in a mother–daughter setup. This was her plan for retirement, timed with my senior year in high school. The last thing I wanted to do was change schools and move away from my friends, especially Bill. But she went, and I went to live with a girlfriend from school, Ann, and her family. Ann lived in the same development as Bill, so I knew the area. Ann moved out of her shared bedroom with her sister, and we set up our bedroom together in their finished basement. We decorated the walls with posters of the day, peace signs, and rock bands we liked. We played Bob Dylan and Donavan and talked until we fell asleep at night.

One night at dinner, I looked around the family dining table. Ann's parents were good, kind, hardworking people. Her father was a builder, a strong, in-charge kind of guy. It was different for me to have a man at the table since it had just been my mother and me. It made me feel kind of secure and fearful at the same time. Her mom was a small, dark-haired woman who seemed to run the house so easily and seamlessly. She was a waitress at Howard Johnson's. She got me a job there as soon as she realized I had no other means of support. My stepmother was not sending any money.

Ann's parents were so generous to open their home to me. They were ordinary people who had done an extraordinary thing in my life. They really didn't know me or my family, and yet they took me in. Ann and her younger sister were both beautiful and very good students. They were well liked at school, senior queen material.

On the other hand, I was "poor Susan."

At that time, I was convinced that everyone saw me as a girl whose parents had both died and who had a wicked stepmother and a family that never saw her. And I was still often sick. Most importantly, "poor Susan" was how I saw myself. Even though my stepmother wasn't sending me any money at the time, growing up, I had not been poor dollar-wise. I had more than most, but I did not see myself as successful or strong. Sitting there at the kitchen table on that particular day, I had a sudden realization: I saw that there was no payoff in being poor Susan, and I wasn't going to live my life that way anymore. I wanted to achieve and to be successful. I would no longer allow my fear to stop me. I would do whatever I needed to do in spite of my fear. Change can take place at a moment's notice, and that day, it did. Without a word or awareness from anyone at the table, I gave birth to a new me. From that moment forward, I lived by mottos like "Fear is excitement without breath" (Fritz Perl) and "Life should be a daring adventure or nothing" (Helen Keller). If something frightened me, I no longer had a choice—I had to do it. I did certain things just to build my character. I was no longer willing to live in fear or to acknowledge the fear that might still reside in me.

As time went on, this decision would lead me to fire walking, parachuting, scuba diving, rock climbing, and many stressful public speaking events. And now my volunteer work in Romania. It wasn't that I was no longer afraid. The fear was still there, calling me as a red cape calls to the bull. But I no longer had the ability to say no just because I was afraid. As the red flag of fear went up, it showed me what I had to do.

Later in life, I realized that this unacknowledged fear still ruled me. I thought I was overcoming my weak image of myself, and in some ways, I was. I tried new things and took many more chances. But there was one area of my life that I couldn't just push through: my personal relationships, especially with Bill. I was told more than once by more than one person that I had a hard edge to me. I couldn't see it at the time, but now I can see how I was unable to let anyone know how much they meant to me. In an argument, I could easily say to someone, "Go, it's okay; I don't care." I told myself I didn't need that person in my life. If I were to show them I cared for them, I would have to admit it to myself. I can even see now that this same long-simmering, long-buried fear also colored my attitude about having children. *If I do, I do. If I don't, I don't.* I never let myself or anyone else know I cared one way or another. The possibility of another loss of the heart was so frightening, it stayed hidden from me. It would take me years to approach this fear. Like a sleeping giant, it had to be tricked into submission—and it was, by a very unlikely group.

Arrival in Romania,
January 1991

I t was dark, very dark, below me as I looked out of the airplane window. It was hard to believe that there was any life below, much less Bucharest, one of Romania's major cities. I was feeling pretty good. My flight over had been easy; I got bumped up to first class and slept most of the way. I thought about how nice it was for the flight attendant to upgrade me when she found out I was going to volunteer. She didn't know that the ticket I was flying on was free after I'd given up my seat the year before when I went to Rome.

This trip is working out for me, I reflected on my good luck.

My thoughts were running wild. *What would I feel like on my return months from now; how would I be changed? How would Romania and the horrid conditions I expected to see affect me? Would I want to stay connected to the program, or would I just want to walk away?*

My focus changed quickly as I overheard the two guys sitting behind me. They were talking about whether they would serve in the army in Iraq if called.

January 15, just two days away, was the deadline set for the pull-out by the Iraqis, or else we would declare war. The media was already using terms like shock and awe, bombardment, and Desert Storm.

When Stephanie and I were at the mall just days ago, small crowds of people were gathered around TV monitors as Secretary of State James Baker spoke about how badly the talks were going. *Oh, great!* I thought. The day of the showdown and a possible war was to be my first day with the children in Romania. I thought of Brother Toby and his emphatic words, "Nothing is going to stop us!" Not that I wanted to stop; I just liked knowing that I had the option, and I was no longer sure I did.

I felt uneasy as I thought, *What would it be like to be away from home with our country at war? How much would I be able to know about it? Would my family and friends be safe?*

When the plane landed in Bucharest, we disembarked onto the tarmac. I was ferociously cold as I crossed the tarmac and felt even more so as I walked past the armed guards directing us into the terminal. I had never seen anyone with a rifle at an airport. In the US, the airport was mostly a fun place to be: a place to greet loved ones; start a vacation; feel the excitement of a business trip, or, better than that, return from a business trip to your loved ones. It was a place where the worst that happened was that the airlines lost your bag or you were delayed, certainly nothing that would require a rifle. I was starting to realize this was not going to be a warm and fuzzy experience. The terminal was made from gray concrete and marble that held on to the cold. The rooms were large and the ceilings were high, further adding to the cold seeping into my bones.

I got through immigration pretty quickly, having shown my many documents. For my six-month visa to be issued, I had to present my passport, letter of intention, and other documents that were given to me by Brother Toby.

On the other side of immigration was such a wonderful sight: Stephanie! She had arrived the day before and managed to get herself through customs. She was collecting my bags and the many boxes of donations I had brought with me. Brother Toby had given her the official title of cellarer (the person in a monastery in charge of provisions), but we thought of her more like King Rat from the 1965 war movie—same idea, just much scabbier. She was at her best that day. It made my head spin how quickly she had us packed up and off to the hotel.

So this is Romania, I thought on our way to the hotel. There was a smell in the air that I associated with Europe. I don't know what it is, maybe a lack of catalytic converters on the cars, the dust, and the coal. During my stay in the country, the exhaust from the cars often bothered me. As I looked out the window, I tried to make out the surrounding area, but it was too dark. It was nearing 6 p.m. on a winter's night, so it *should* have been dark, but this was a dark I didn't know. The few street lights were dim, and the homes we passed had a single light shining. Not at all like my house, which was usually lit up like a Christmas tree. I don't know what I'd been expecting, but I hadn't given much thought to how little light there would be. I found it annoying that nothing looked clear to me. I wanted to get a good sense of where I was. A short year and a half ago, I would hardly have been able to pick Romania out on the map; now, I was here for the next few months for the most intimate and emotional of undertakings. I wanted to see my way, literally and figuratively. I hoped that the daylight tomorrow would bring that clarity.

I first learned of the Romanian revolution that had taken place two years prior, in 1989, when Bill and I had traveled to Rome for Christmas. At the hotel in Rome, we could only get one station in English, CNN. As we were getting dressed for Christmas dinner, we had the news on in the background. On the TV, a man and woman stood in front of a cement wall; they looked like they were husband and wife. They appeared to be in their seventies, and he was taller and more formidable than her. Both wore business clothes. He had his hat on, and she wore a scarf tied under her chin, as a woman from the country would wear. She was yelling at someone, seeming to scold them. Then, as we tried to understand what was happening, the couple was riddled with bullets. They were shot and killed, and it was televised. Shocked, we read the crawler across the bottom of the screen, which told us this was Nicolae Ceaușescu, the president of Romania, and his wife, Elena.

I wondered what kind of a country could shoot their president on live television. Maybe today, post-9/11, it isn't so unfathomable, but back then it was unimaginable. Since CNN was our only resource for news, we unwillingly caught the scene time and time again until it was etched in our heads. Even today, so many years later, I can still see it and feel the confusion as I tried to make sense of what I saw on that holiest of evenings, Christmas.

Stephanie and I were staying at a hotel in the center of Bucharest. It wasn't a large hotel but more like a country inn, resembling a thatched cottage. I quickly changed and joined my small group of volunteers—Stephanie, Chuck, Sarah, and Brother Toby—for dinner. This evening was to be my first impression of life in Romania.

I walked into a cold, dark, smoky room of mostly men, who sat at tables smoking and drinking with their fur hats and coats on. It was like a scene from the movie *Reds* and the Eastern Front. The food was so bad that I almost thought it was a joke. We could not cut our meat, and the other items on our plates were bland and cold. Our group was mystified when the waiter asked what we would like to eat and drink. We then went through a ritual that I would learn was very common in Romania's better restaurants. First you pretend that you have a choice of entrees on the extensive menu that you have been handed. Then, when the waiter asks for your order, you begin by asking for your desired dish, only to be told, "Sorry, we do not have that item this evening." Then it's your turn to ask for something else. This dance goes on until you grow frustrated and ask, "Well, what *do* you have?" to which the waiter responds, "Chicken or pork."

This exchange made me laugh every time it happened. I couldn't understand why the waiter didn't start by saying we only have chicken or pork this evening and it is cooked only one way, the chef's way. My best guess as to why this inefficient practice continued is because it came from a more prosperous time when food and drink were more plentiful.

I remember thinking, *I am going to starve in this country.*

Thankfully, that first meal turned out to be the worst meal I had during my stay.

The Romanians care a lot about their food and make wonderful dishes, often from very little. One of my favorite dishes was eggplant salad and country bread served as an accompaniment to chorba (a soup). This soup is the pride of every cook. I can't say what the soup is made from because every time I had it, it was different, but it was always called chorba.

That night, I went to bed thinking about Bill, missing him, and imagining that it must be much harder for him than for me. He was home in his usual routine, coming home to an empty house while I was having this amazing adventure. It didn't seem fair that only I was having this experience. Before I left, as we held on to each other one night, we spoke about how our marriage felt strong enough to endure this time apart.

That even though we would be apart, we were in this together. We felt so blessed with each other, family, and friends; we wanted to extend ourselves and help others. I fell asleep feeling peaceful, comforted, and warmed by these thoughts in a freezing hotel room on my first night in Romania.

The next day we had a morning meeting with Brother Toby. He gave us his talk on death and dying. We had heard that this talk was coming, so anticipation ran high. The film crew from *Primetime Live*, who were following the story, were with us for it. I don't know if it fit the bill for either group since it turned out to be one of Toby's shortest, but his few words stuck with me. In a nutshell, he said, "Our job is not to worry about the dying. Our job is to tend to the living; the dying will take care of itself."

Over the years, there have been many times that these simple words have shown me the way and helped me deal with the sickness of others and the fear that can come with caring for those in their final days.

After our morning meeting, we were off to Constanta, a three-hour drive from Bucharest through small villages on bumpy roads. It was slow going since we had to deal with one-lane roads with huge potholes, slow-moving tractors, and horse-drawn wagons. By the time we finally got to Constanta and Post Cura #4, it was getting dark outside.

Post Cura #4 looked a lot like the army barracks that were across the street from it. The two-story, gray stucco building with bars on the windows offered nothing inviting to the visitor. No one would guess that the gray gravel path from the road to the door would take you to sixty babies and toddlers on the other side. It was not a place that beckoned you to get out of the cold. In fact, just looking at it made you feel chilled.

Post Cura #4 was established under the Municipal Hospital in Constanta. Dr. Matusa was the head of Pediatric Infectious Diseases at the municipal hospital, so Post Cura #4 came under her authority.

In Romania, in 1989, the general stance of the communist government was that HIV/AIDS didn't exist. Later, Romania would have the highest number of infected children in Europe. It was hard to take care of something that didn't exist.

Dr. Matusa said, "I had to go, monthly, to the Health Directorate where the cases of child mortality were discussed, and we, the doctors and the medical staff, were generally reprimanded for not doing our job like the world, and that's why children were dying."

However, Dr. Matusa knew this was not the case. It was only after Ceaușescu's death that the virus was finally acknowledged in Romania.

In December 1990, Dr. Matusa visited Brother Toby at Starcross and saw the normal life that their four HIV-positive children were living. She saw how this family model gave the children the rights every child deserves: to be cared for, nurtured, and loved. The model of care for the children impressed her, so together with Brother Toby, she sought permission from the Ministry of Health to take over a building in Constanta that was being secretly used to house HIV-positive babies. These children were being warehoused, with only medical professionals allowed to enter the building. Most children were kept there until the age of two. If they survived past that age, they would be moved to another facility for older children.

When Starcross took over the building, we renamed it Casa Speranta (House of Hope). We immediately set the children up in the family model.

As Dr. Matusa said, "The strong impression left on us by foreign volunteers, who came and made us follow their example, was overwhelming. From them, we learned not to leave the children in bed and to take them in our arms; from them, we learned that they must be well fed, that they must be educated."

This model of care proved to be all that we had hoped for in improving the children's health and general well-being. Moreover, it was a model of care that other not-for-profit organizations acknowledged and followed.

On the other side of the front door, the building's drab coolness continued into the hallway. To the left was a small room with an old easy chair and a child's table and chair. The room was used for visits from the children's family members. It was not used often. Across from it was a room with half-glass walls. The room was dimly lit and eerily quiet. I wondered if there were children sleeping there. Diagonally across from that room and behind the visitors' room was another room with half-glass walls, where a couple of women were sitting and smoking. This, I was to learn, was the head nurse's office. The walls were painted gray, as was the rest of the building. Inside and out, there was nothing welcoming about Post Cura #4. But Stephanie and I didn't care as we unloaded our suitcases and the many boxes of donations. We only had one thing on our minds: what we had come for, the children.

Moving into our designated apartments and learning the layout of the building and wards where the children resided is all sort of a blur now. I don't remember specific conversations with the other volunteers or with the nurses. I don't really remember who was doing what. I do remember going up the concrete steps that led to where we would be staying and quickly trying to imagine living with the children in this cold, dark place.

As Stephanie and I walked into the ward of sleeping kids, however, we looked at each other and immediately embraced as we simultaneously said, "Home." This place, cold and dark a moment ago, had changed; the faces of the twenty or so children had changed it for us.

I cautiously approached one of the toddlers. He, or was it she? It was hard to tell since all children had shaven heads to keep the lice down. I'm not someone who walks into a room and scoops up a child, as I notice many people do. I admire a person's confidence in that approach, but it's not me. So I spoke with this boy with big brown eyes and allowed him to check me out before

I picked him up. His body felt warm, but his hands were cold around my neck. He played with my ponytail as I moved around the room. He was dressed in what looked to be new PJs that were bulging with cloths under them; I guessed this was some kind of diaper to keep him dry. I looked around the room for a blanket; there weren't any.

Now I started to notice more of my surroundings, the grayish look of the room and the heavy smell of antiseptic. I wondered how I hadn't heard the calls of "Mama, Mama" that filled the room. This call was not coming from one child but from many. I could see their little hands reaching out of their cribs, hoping, wanting, needing to be picked up. *It's not possible*, I thought. *How can I or anyone meet the needs of so many?*

I wanted to walk away from the pain of what I was seeing, but I knew I could never do that. These were the children I had come here to help. This is how they had lived their lives—most were rocking, some were rubbing their mouths back and forth on metal cribs (likely covered with lead paint), and others were staring blankly. Because these children had been infected with the AIDS virus, they were left here to die.

I now realized that this child I was carrying and who was holding me tightly would need to be put back down. Even though this was the very same image that had moved me when I'd first seen Brother Toby on *Primetime Live*, I wasn't prepared for it. *How will I be able to set him down?* It suddenly struck me there was another part to this situation that I hadn't realized when watching Brother Toby. Not only did the child not want to let go, but I didn't want to either.

Luckily, my bracelet interested him and he played with that as I put him down. As I slowly left his side, he gave the weakest of cries, a cry that said to me, "It's useless." At that moment, I wished it had been a howl, an angry cry, because that was what I was feeling—anger at a world where this could happen to these babies. On my way out of the ward, my eyes met Stephanie's. I knew from the tears running down her cheeks neither of us could speak; what could we say?

I decided that it was best to stay busy, but my thoughts were still with the children. *How do I go back? How do I not go back? How can I pick up or comfort just one?* As my thoughts continued, I walked into my new apartment. It was easy to find since the whole floor was pretty barren. Chuck had just created three small rooms by putting up temporary walls made from sheetrock. Prior to Chuck's work, this area had been another ward, and like the others, it was about eight hundred square feet, the size of a studio apartment. One wall was half glass so that caregivers could look in on the children without needing to enter. There were two of these large rooms on each floor. I wondered where the children had gone. I could tell they had been there recently from the cribs that were stacked up in the hall. My guess was that they had been moved to another post cura.

These three rooms were to be mine, as I was to receive the first family. On the other side of the hall, there was a room used for making formula and washing bottles, a storage room packed with stuffed toys that were never distributed, and clothes and shoes that these children never got to wear. I learned that this area would be turned into an apartment for Stephanie's family.

Stephanie and I quickly went about setting up four of the cribs in one of the rooms in my apartment; the other room had our beds and one crib. The third room was for the children to eat and play. The apartment felt spacious, but it was not going to be just mine for long. The next day, when Dr. Matusa arrived, she instructed us to make it into two apartments. We needed to make room for more children. As a post cura, the building housed sixty children in cribs packed side by side. Now that the children were to be out of their beds, playing, eating together, with a mom for each family, the building could only take thirty children. The remaining thirty were moved to other facilities.

Stephanie and I finished making up the children's beds, putting away the donations, and making a list of supplies that Stephanie, as our cellarer, would obtain the next day. We were exhausted and excited; tomorrow, we would be taking the first children out of the ward. We both slept well through the night until we were awakened by an early-morning knock on the door. It was the producer from *Primetime Live*. She was clearly upset. On the way over from her hotel, she had learned that our country had gone to war with Iraq. There had been bombings during the night, and she and her team were very concerned about their friends and associates who were covering the story.

This was the beginning of the first Desert Storm, and although I had been following the conflict, in the previous twenty-four hours, I hadn't been giving too much thought to world affairs. This news of war took me by surprise. My mind immediately went to what this might mean for my new family of children in Romania. What did it mean for me? Would they be safe? Would I be safe? I felt so vulnerable being out of the US when it was at war. I had gone to bed the night before feeling like a kid on Christmas Eve, filled with joyful anticipation. Now, that excitement was coupled with apprehension and fear. This feeling filled the space of our new home that day. Like a ping-pong match, our emotions got thrown back and forth as we welcomed the children to their new home and missed the security of being at home with our loved ones.

Soon after the *Primetime Live* producers arrived, a call came from Brother Toby, who was staying at a nearby hotel. I picked up the clunky black phone from the receiver to hear him say, "Susan, are you ready for the children—to receive your family?"

Switching gears away from the news of the war, I excitedly told him, "I'm more than ready; it feels like Christmas morning."

Brother Toby arrived in short order and was eager to get the children from the wards that were downstairs and across the hall. Because only one apartment was ready, we would only be able to take five children today. The rest would need to wait. Chuck was moving fast, but when it came to children living like animals, it is never fast enough.

Brother Toby had been waiting for this day since his first trip to Romania. The film crew was ready; the apartment was ready, and I was ready. The volunteers, Brother Toby, and I joined in a circle as Brother Toby blessed us and asked me again—for the film crew—if I was ready.

One by one, I took each child from the ward downstairs and brought them upstairs to our apartment. The first was brown-eyed, blonde-haired, two-year-old Ionel. He was dressed in grayish pants and a shirt, with many layers of cloth around him. I felt the heaviness of the wet cloth; there were no cloth diapers or Pampers to be found in Romania. Ionel was so cute and excited, standing in his crib, happy and eager to get out. He immediately put his hands up, much to my relief. Ionel was clearly ready, and from that moment on, he would become the leader of our family. I brought him up the cold gray stairs into his new apartment and home. Brother Toby greeted him, and then Stephanie and Sarah got him changed as I went to bring the next child up, TV cameras in tow.

Next, from the crib adjacent to Ionel, was three-and-a-half-year-old Ramona. She also had brown eyes but darker hair and skin, and she was bigger and more verbal than Ionel. However, I had no idea what she was saying. I think it was just babbling, but she was very excited as she expressed herself. She also had no reluctance at being picked up and carried upstairs by a strange person with a camera crew.

When I got her upstairs, we took her old hospital garb off and dressed her, as Ionel now was, in Princeton orange sweats. They came from home, and the children loved the tigers on them. Ramona waddled around the room as she checked out her new home, babbling all the while. She would never stop being the talker.

Next, I went to get one-and-a-half-year-old, blonde-haired, blue-eyed Mihaela. I could tell she was blonde even though her head had been shaven like all of the children's. She was also willing to come with me, a stranger, although she seemed a little cautious as she looked around.

As she entered the apartment, Brother Toby blessed her as he had blessed each child with the prayer:

Dear God, here is your child, Mihaela
Put your star in her heart and allow her
To walk with you today and every day of her life.

After the first three children arrived, we had some extra time because the nurses told us that the next two were napping. The volunteers—Chuck, Stephanie, Sarah, and I—sat around on the carpeted floor playing with the children the way we had longed to since starting this program. Brother Toby watched over us, took some video, and I think relished the fact that there were at least a few babies out of a horrible situation and starting to live life.

Then it was baby Costin's turn. Costin was one year old, the youngest but not the smallest. He was so cute; as he grabbed onto my neck, he rested his head on my shoulder. I felt him relax in my arms as if he felt that he was finally safe. I realized as I put him down that he, like Mihaela, was not yet walking. So when I put him on the floor, he crawled to sit on Stephanie's lap. I would learn he was always his happiest when physically attached.

Last came Dana-Rica. This child was very special to Brother Toby. It was on his first trip to Romania that Brother Toby walked into a ward, silent aside from one child laughing: Dana-Rica. He picked up this tiny little girl with a huge smile, and when he went to put her down, she wouldn't let go physically or emotionally. His heart broke as he assessed the situation and promised her he would help her as best he could. When he returned to the United States, she haunted him every day and every night; she represented the children in Romania that needed help so badly. He needed to return to these children, and her frail image was there not to let him forget; it filled him with a sense of urgency, letting him know that every minute of every day was a matter of life and death for these children.

As our group stood in a circle with Dana-Rica, Dr. Matusa asked us, "Are you sure you want to take her? She's very sick and will only bring you problems."

We answered in spontaneous unison, "We will take her."

The Romanians were trying to avoid problems with these first children; they wanted this new project to look successful. If these first children didn't survive for long, it wouldn't bode well for the project. We'd been given this building and these children to care for by the Municipal Hospital in Constanta. It was our job to show that when the children were given a chance to live, their lives and health would improve. We would show the hospital system and whoever else was interested that, HIV or no HIV, every child deserves the right to live a normal life surrounded by people that love them.

But it was not even a question if I was going to take Dana-Rica. She meant too much to Brother Toby, and he wasn't going to turn his back on her just because she was ill. That day when I took her from the ward, she weighed only eight pounds at two and a half years old. She couldn't sit up, talk, roll over, or eat with a spoon. She was like an infant.

As Brother Toby blessed her, he looked deep into her eyes and said, "I told you I would be back, and look what I brought you."

It was me!

HIV/AIDS

In 1990–1991, Romania and the US were years apart in their understanding of the AIDS virus. Romania's position was not hard to understand since, under Ceauşescu, AIDS was not even acknowledged as a problem; it didn't exist! Those who were found to have contracted this nonexistent virus were stored away in buildings such as Post Cura #4. The employees in these human warehouses were sworn to secrecy, not even allowed to speak with their families about their patients' condition. In buildings like Casa Speranta, children were left to die.

Romania had primarily pediatric HIV infections, whereas, in the US, it was predominately adults. In Romania, contaminated blood was said to have entered the country through the seaport, where sailors sold their blood. Children in Romania contracted the virus from unsafe medical practices like reusing needles and transfusing contaminated blood. After Ceauşescu's death, the number of children found to be infected in Romania was overwhelming. I was shocked when I visited the municipal hospital to find seventy children admitted. This was a sharp contrast to the San

Francisco hospital treating Tina, where two children were admitted to the infectious disease ward.

In 1990, the United States had a long way to go with our acceptance and treatment of AIDS, but we had started research to find a cure. Government and non-government organizations had begun to tackle the problems associated with HIV/AIDS. Along with the need to find the right medication to treat the disease, patients suffered extreme alienation from fear and prejudice. These problems needed to be addressed through awareness and education. In Romania, research and medication weren't considered necessary, since the disease didn't officially exist. The United States had a few drugs on the market to combat the disease; Romania had none.

In the United States, a few influential people started speaking out about contracting the virus. Elizabeth Glaser (wife of actor Paul Glaser) was one of the first. She had contracted the virus during childbirth when she needed a transfusion. Elizabeth unknowingly passed it on to her children. She spoke out at the 1992 Democratic National Convention to appeal to lawmakers to support research to find a cure that would save her children and others like them. Unfortunately, neither she nor her daughter, Ariel, would be given enough time to receive the life-saving medication that resulted from her efforts.

Ryan White also gave a face to this dreaded disease. He was a young boy who received the virus through a blood transfusion when he was thirteen. When his HIV status was revealed, Ryan faced extreme opposition from his community. Many did not want him to attend school for fear that he would infect their children. The fear was so strong at one point that someone shot a bullet into his house. However, Ryan's story caught the attention of many celebrities, who came out in support of him. He and his family started to bring awareness to HIV/AIDS and to educate the public that the disease was not passed through casual contact. Ryan became a strong activist for others who had the disease, and his influence continued even after his death at age eighteen.

Basketball star Magic Johnson publicly announced his HIV status while I was in Romania. This brave decision reassured me that awareness of this disease was rising in the US. Public declarations like Magic's went a long way in getting HIV/AIDS accepted by the general public in the US. But, make no mistake, the US had a long way to go in finding a way to manage this deadly disease. The significant difference between the US and Romania was that in Romania, AIDS had yet to even be acknowledged.

The Woman Who
Lived in a Shoe

I was now the ex-officio mother to five children, and I was overwhelmed and truly felt like the woman who lived in a shoe. My need to be constantly watching, tidying, orchestrating, feeding, washing, dressing, and lulling to sleep put me in a kind of blur where it was hard to tell where one day ended and another began. The children were so cute and responded well to their newfound life, but I had so much to learn about being a mother to five. These children had lived with so little and needed so much.

I needed to start with the basics. *How do I keep them warm when there's so little heat?* I asked myself. I would have to learn how to swaddle them better and more quickly. I wasn't making much progress with my swaddling attempts. Over half the time, the diaper would fall off after only a few minutes. And since there were no rubber pants, I was back at it almost as soon as I was done with the last child. Dana-Rica was small and not that hard to swaddle, but Ramona was thirty pounds, and flipping her over without losing the fabric wasn't easy. Without rubber pants, trying to keep them dry was futile, but it was the only way right now.

I also needed to be sure that they were getting enough food. I noticed that Dana-Rica was losing much of her bottle because she couldn't hold on to it properly. I would need to feed her myself and speak to the kitchen about getting a better bottle. These plans were just the beginning of meeting their needs, along with giving them the other essentials of love and touch.

I quickly learned how different each child's needs were, but addressing them all was a challenge. How was I to care for all the children and find the time and place to meet each child's specific needs? By the end of the first week, this is what I had learned about the children:

Ramona, three and a half, had spent her entire life inside her crib and only took food through a bottle; no one had taken the time to teach her to eat from a spoon. All bottles were delivered to the apartment in a large pot from the downstairs kitchen. Since Ramona was an older and larger child, she received three bottles at each meal. She also had not been potty trained or taught to speak. But Ramona was a curious, loving child, interested in what everyone was doing, and had a lot to say in her preverbal discourse. She called me and all the women in the building "Mama." This expression was typical of any child who had spent much time in the ward. When someone would enter the room, all the children's hands would go up as they exclaimed, "Mama, Mama." I'd never get used to this heartbreaking sound.

Ramona had learned to walk but had never been outside. The first time we took her outside (or, more accurately, tried to take her out), Ramona ran down the inside stairs with great anticipation. Clearly, she thought that something fun was up, but as we reached the door, she slowed down. As the other children and I continued out into the fresh air, Ramona hung back, sticking her little shaven head out from behind the door to check things out. She wanted so badly to come with us, but her fear held on to her; I could hear it in her laugh. Each time we encouraged her, Ramona would advance a little further out the door onto the concrete steps. She was making real progress until her feet came down off the cement step and touched the grass. The feel of the grass sent her into a panic. Ramona ran back inside before anyone could reach her to let her know that it was okay. It took several more attempts on our part and hers until she was comfortable with this new thing—nature.

At two and a half, **Ionel** had spent the longest time at home with his family before being sent to the ward. And for that reason, he was clearly more advanced than the other children. Unlike Ramona, he had been institutionalized for only one year. Ionel walked, ate with a spoon, and seemed to understand directions. He had a pleasant disposition, although he would wake during the night crying and angry, unable to be consoled.

Bleary-eyed from long, busy days, I would take him out of his crib and try to comfort him. But I had no idea what I was trying to comfort him from. The children were given to us to care for, but we had very little information about them. We'd been given a small blue book with each child's name, birth date, and some medical information. It was not enough to help me understand what upset Ionel in the middle of the night.

Later in my stay, Ionel's mom would share how she learned that Ionel had the virus. She told me that one evening an ambulance came to her house and took the family to the hospital, including herself, her husband, two of Ionel's brothers, and Ionel. They were all tested, and not too long afterward, the father and the two boys were sent home, leaving her and Ionel at the hospital with a group of other mothers and their respective children.

Ionel's mother explained that at the time, the doctors and nurses at the hospital had suspected Ionel might have the secret disease because he had recently been to the clinic with flu-like symptoms. After many days passed in the hospital, during which rumors spread about the new disease that had no cure, the mothers were all called to the doctor's office, where they were told about SIDA (AIDS). The doctor said that they should leave their children at the hospital because if the moms took them home, they would infect them and the other family members; they should consider them dead. This happened when Ionel was just six months old.

So I let Ionel scream as I held him and tried to comfort him with words, words of a foreign language. I had so little to offer him. My only solace was knowing that holding him meant he was one step up from how he had been living in the ward.

Early on, Ionel liked to learn, especially from books. Often I would see him sitting in a corner or the middle of the floor with his new siblings playing around him as he looked at a picture book, totally unaware of their presence. Or he would come to me, plop himself down on my lap, and want me to show him a book. Ionel could concentrate for longer periods of time than the other children.

Dana-Rica, at two and a half, weighed only eight pounds and could not walk, crawl, or sit on her own. Like Ramona, Dana-Rica also had spent her entire life inside a crib. This little brown-haired, brown-eyed pixie had an engaging smile and would laugh easily. However, she had a lot of growing and strengthening to do if she was going to survive.

To strengthen her legs, I put her in a bouncy chair that hung in the middle of the apartment doorway. She loved this chair. I think it was the first time in her life that she was in an upright position since she hadn't been able to sit independently. I believe that this chair went a long way in aiding her development and the extreme progress that she began to make. It strengthened her underdeveloped legs so much that in six months, she could walk. Because of her new upright position, she developed skills necessary for a child to learn, like banging on a hard surface and eye-hand coordination. Also, from this new upright posture, she could now engage with the other children and me. She started to make more precise sounds; she was on her way to talking.

All her progress was unbelievable and seen as a blessing, but there was something more about this child that is difficult to put into words. It must have been the experience that Brother Toby had when he first met her and couldn't forget. She had this capacity to make me laugh when I needed to the most. She also seemed to have this preternatural ability to take care of those around her even without having the physical strength to do so. This feeling that she sparked in me seemed to come from somewhere else. On my darkest days, time with her could heal my soul.

Mihaela, at one-and-a-half years old, took off walking the first day we got her out of her crib. This blonde, blue-eyed little nymph seemed like she had just been waiting for someone to say go. From the moment she walked, she was very active and fearless. She was not very interested in what the other children were doing or in joining them.

Mihaela stayed on the perimeter of the room. She seemed to have a problem with her hearing, which might have been the cause of her distancing herself. She also had not been trained to eat from a spoon. Her adenoids were so large I wondered if it was even possible for her to eat solid food. This active daredevil needed an additional hour longer than the others at the end of each day to settle down so she could sleep. This timing difference was hard on me because when the children's bedtime came around, I was exhausted. Mihaela's difficulty going to sleep made me even wearier. In her struggle to settle down, she would get the other kids going. I'm pretty sure she was the ringleader the week they all learned to climb out of their cribs. Even Dana-Rica got out of the crib with the help of the other children. This was not what I had in mind when I wanted them to bond with each other.

Costin was just one year old and, by all rights, the baby of the group. He was taller and larger than Dana-Rica since she was just eight hundred grams at birth and had a lot of catching up to do. Costin could sit, crawl, and stand with support, but emotionally, he was not a happy child. He had constant diarrhea and was clingy and whiny. As with Ionel, I often did not know what I could do to make him more comfortable. He was always attached to my hip; he needed reassurance, and this is where he got it. On the rare days that he had energy, he played well with the other children. Baths made him squeal with joy, as did a food that he really liked. It became a family thing when someone especially liked their food; they would wriggle the way Costin did. We all called it "the Costin wiggle."

But Costin never seemed to be feeling well. As days went by, I became more and more convinced that his virus was active. The other children seemed to be stronger than Costin.

They all got herpes zosters and had molluscum (a wart-like virus). Mihaela had constant ear infections and needed to have her swollen adenoids removed, but no doctor wanted to operate on a child with SIDA. Unlike Costin's, Mihaela's problems could be identified. Costin had an overall presentation of poor health.

In these early days of the virus, HIV/AIDS was like an unwelcome guest that appeared differently each time, trying to gain entry into our lives. We never knew how or where this villain would get our children, but we had little doubt that it was coming for them. We had seen its presence. With the children, a cold was never just a cold, a rash was never just a rash, and a cough was not just a cough. We looked at these symptoms in fear that maybe this time AIDS had gotten in to hurt and take our children from us.

The kids were on a drug called Septrum, prophylactically, to keep infections down. But the drug had come from the US, and like many of our donations, it was outdated. So we questioned whether it was making any difference. A doctor came to make rounds every few days or so, or we could bring the children to the hospital if needed. Otherwise, the "mothers" ran back and forth between apartments asking each other what they knew about the symptoms that were bothering their child and what they might do about them.

During these days, I also needed to learn about Romania and how different life was here than in the States. Romania felt dark to me. We lived on a busy street where many people walked by our building on their way to the tram and back to their homes. Nothing was uplifting in this parade of people. Even their body posture, heads down and shoulders hunched forward, implied a hard life. I was learning so much about what life had been like for them not that long ago under Ceaușescu. I hoped that I wasn't projecting unhappiness on them. I learned that the Securitate, the secret police established under Ceaușescu, was very real to them. Because of this, it wasn't safe to speak negatively about the government even to your closest neighbor. In fact, according to the Securitate's own archives, an estimated 750,000 people out of a population of 23 million collaborated with the secret police. But the belief was that it was much higher. In a 2009 *Independent* article, Oana Lungescu, a Romanian citizen, described the hold of the Securitate over the Romanian people this way:

> *As the regime entered its final decade, people had been cowed into thinking the secret police was*

*all-powerful. The Securitate controlled us through our own fear.**

As an American, I came into this situation believing that anything was possible; if I encountered an obstacle, I'd simply look for another way until I got what I wanted. In Romania, the general stance was, "It's not possible." One of the first Romanian words I learned was *de ce,* or "why?"

"De ce, can't I get another bottle of milk for Dana-Rica?"

"De ce, can't I go to the store and buy diaper rash cream for Mihaela?"

"De ce, can't I get one cushy chair for the apartment where the children and I could sit?"

In the next few days, I would come to understand "de ce." But for now, it was becoming apparent that I had a lot to learn about Romania and my new living situation.

Meanwhile, my relationship with the other volunteers wasn't going well; tension was high, and we were all stressed out, making life feel more difficult. We were all feeling the pressure of getting this project going and getting used to our new living environment and the frustrations that it brought. Each day we would wake up only to find that life at Casa Speranta had served us

---

* Oana Lungescu, "Romania's Revolution: The Day I Read My Secret Police File," *The Independent,* December 11, 2009, *https://www.independent.co.uk/news/world/europe/romanias-revolution-the-day-i-read-my-secret-police-file-1838206.html.*

another challenge. Usually, heat, or lack of it, greeted us at sunrise. Wrapped in blankets, I would go into the children's room only to find them soaking wet and chilled from the night. I didn't know what to do first. Did I do like they say on airplanes—help myself first, then take care of those who cannot help themselves? That meant getting dressed and warming myself before I helped the crying children get warm. Whichever I chose, all I thought about the whole time was getting footie PJs for the kids from the US as fast as I could. Changing the children meant using cold water to clean them. . . . No heat, no hot water. When I put the cold rag on their bottoms, they cringed—or, in Dana-Rica's case, literally screamed. It bothered her so much that when we passed the centrally located sink, even when I had no intention of washing her, she would start hollering.

In addition to our hot water and heat problem, many days, we had neither water nor electricity. For a day or two, we felt like pioneers, but after that, things would feel tense. The best part was when we got the services back, usually one at a time, and we felt for a while like we had everything we needed.

Although our group of volunteers got on each other's nerves, we were able to sit down together, work out our differences, and move forward. This ability was not something that later groups of volunteers had.

My biggest problem with the other volunteers in those early days was expecting them to lend me a hand since I was the only one with children. I think if I had done less expecting and more asking, I might have gotten the help I needed. Also, everything I did felt hard since I wasn't feeling well. I was so tired of hearing myself say, "I just don't feel well." I was embarrassed to hear myself constantly complain; this was not my usual behavior. I had a constant cold with the worst runny nose, with no tissues and sometimes no toilet paper. This meant the children's cloths for diapering were my only recourse.

But for me, the children made any difficulty worthwhile. I think this was also true for the other volunteers, who would stop by to get their fix from the children. They came to visit my family since their apartments weren't ready yet. Since we had no furniture, only an area carpet, the floor is where we spent our time. It was fun to play with these active children and watch them interact with each other. While I was on the floor watching the children, I had a subtle but powerful experience.

It was two or so weeks into my time with the children, as I watched them from my place on the floor, when it occurred to me that I had a choice. I could completely and entirely open myself up to them, or love them but hold a part of myself back. Since I was a volunteer, I would be leaving in just three months, and so I could shield myself from the anticipated pain of loss. Or I could just allow myself to open up to them—to love them unconditionally and take a chance that I would be able to handle our painful goodbyes.

Just then, one of the boys came over and snuggled into my lap. My decision became physical: I felt my whole body open up like a flower that just popped into full bloom. Suddenly, I knew what was right for me; I was going for it.

My heart had been closed for such a long time, if not my entire life. I'd needed this to protect me and help me deal with the loneliness and loss in my life. Now my heart had opened; it was leading me, and I felt like there was no going back. Until that moment, I hadn't realized how much I wanted and needed this connection between a mother and child. In the past, I had spoken of wanting a child but hadn't known what that meant. At this moment, I knew what it meant and allowed myself to open, knowing it would only be for a few short months. I was opening myself up to love and the inevitable pain that goes with choosing to be a mother. It was not until this moment that I realized the pain that a woman chooses when she decides to have a child. Pain that she may not even acknowledge to herself, much less put into words. How could I possibly hold myself back when these kids were so open, loving, and trusting of me? As they had languished in their cribs, they had been waiting for this connection—someone to love and to love them back—and I was not going to deny them or myself this opportunity.

Trip to Town

Chuck helped me place a call to the US to speak with Bill. Calling home was a complicated process that included using my not nearly good enough Romanian. There was only one phone in the building, and it was located in a small entranceway to Chuck's room. It wasn't possible to place a call directly; the Romanian international operator had to place it. Often it would take hours before the operator would get the connection. It was such a long process, and when I finally got through, I was so nervous that I would get cut off; I could hardly remember all that I wanted to say.

But on that day, hearing Bill's voice was just what I needed. This first week with the children had been so full and fulfilling, but I couldn't understand why I still wasn't feeling well. I felt like I had never gotten my strength back from the really bad cold/flu I got when I was at the hospital with Tina. Not feeling well was dragging me down.

I knew I had woken Bill when I heard his sleepy voice.

"Susan? Oh good, it's you; how are you?" I could tell he had been sound asleep and was trying to pull his thoughts together. This was our first call since I'd arrived in Constanta; we'd spoken only briefly on my first night in Bucharest.

"Tell me what's it like," Bill said, as he tried so hard to wake himself.

"The children are great—I wish you could meet them," I said, suddenly realizing, with the seven-hour difference, it was about 3 a.m. for him.

"Oh, Bill," I exclaimed, "I'm so sorry. I placed this call so long ago, I didn't realize the time."

"I don't care," he said. "Tell me the children's names."

What seemed like an easy question after a week with the children wasn't that easy. "Ramona," I said with no problem, then Ionel, who everyone called Ionut, a nickname for Ionel. I faked that one. Dana-Rica, I couldn't seem to remember; in Romanian, Dana is pronounced "Donna." Then Mihaela, who I wanted to call Micaela (my niece's name), and finally Constantine, shortened to Costin, which is pronounced "Costine."

After stumbling over their names for a few minutes, I gave him a quick rundown of our daily life and complained about how bad I felt. I said with frustration, "I need to call you another time. It's late. I feel bad waking you, and the connection is really bad. I just wish you could come here. I need to go," I said, almost in tears. "I love you."

"Susan! Susan! Wait!" I heard him yell. "I'm coming to Romania on March 15. I made reservations today."

"Really?" I cried. "You did? But what about the expense? Aren't the tickets expensive?" I asked.

"I have my free ticket from giving up our seats when we went to Rome. It's all set; I'm coming," he said.

This was the best news. As we hung up to a million I love yous, I had tears in my eyes and maybe even just a moment of not feeling sick.

* * *

Aside from my malaise and lack of energy, life with the children was going really well. We were getting a routine down. The children were eating, getting outside, and sleeping. Putting them to bed was easy; they were used to that. It was the days that were more challenging as I tried to create routines and fun activities for the kids. I was learning quickly what I could and couldn't expect from two one-year-olds, two two-year-olds, and a three-year-old.

Getting the children outside became one of my priorities.

In one of the storage rooms, I found an old two-seater carriage, in which I put Costin and Mihaela. Mihaela was a very new walker, and Costin was still on all fours, so I was happy to find this means of transporting them. Ramona and Ionel waddled as they walked but did pretty well at keeping up as they hung on to either side of the carriage. Dana-Rica was in a backpack on my back. She was so small I hardly knew she was there. With this setup, all six of us could hit the road.

One day, I decided to take us all on a trip to town so we could go to the market and the park. A small market was just blocks away, and I was eager to get the kids out and also to see what was available for sale.

Walking down the city street, we passed a school-yard; the class yelled out words that they thought, as an American, I would know, like "Texas!" or "Dallas!" Many Romanians, especially children, thought everyone in America lived like J. R. Ewing. This belief was responsible for some of the problems we were beginning to have with the Romanian staff, who assumed that as Americans we had more than we needed. The staff had begun to take things from our apartments or from the donations we had been sent. Although it made me crazy to return to my room sometimes to find my only light bulb missing, it was hard to get too angry. Life had gotten pretty bleak when you needed to steal a light bulb.

We walked past apartment block after apartment block lining the street. This was Ceaușescu's handi-work. He had taken private property away from individuals and replaced their homes with lookalike gray concrete buildings. Since the coup a year earlier, people were now starting to apply to get their family properties back. I heard it was quite a challenge for the court system to work out a property's ownership from decades before.

The children and I came to the main corner of our district, Kilometer 45, where the outside market was located. The children were interested in everything around them, and everyone around us was interested in us; one mom with five kids wasn't a common sight. There were only a few tables set up. One table had only a few flowers for sale, and another table had one bundle of carrots. Just one bundle! Coupled with a few poorly stocked stores, this was the market. Up the street, I could see a long line of people. I knew from Stephanie that this was the bread line. In days to come, if I saw a line like that, I would quickly investigate since there was so little available to buy. It was best to stop what you were doing and get whatever was being sold because there was no knowing when you might see that product again.

Next, we went to the park. It wasn't much of a park, but it was a park. I made a note to myself to return with one of the other volunteers so that I could let the older children run. I wasn't ready or able to let two toddlers run when I had three that were not yet walking. The park had probably been nice in the seventies. I could see that there had been a fountain, which was now all dried up with grass growing through the cracked concrete. There was concrete on the ground where a swing set and jungle gym might have been. There was still a seesaw that was a little broken but still worked, and a slide. This would be a great place for the kids to get some exercise. I pointed out to the children the man with the goat who was doing the job of being a natural lawn mower. Every once in a while, I would see this same man and his goat dining at Casa Speranta.

On our adventure, an older man from the neighborhood stopped us and said, "Bravo." I understood through our made-up sign language that he was happy to see the children out and wanted to say thank you for my help. He seemed to be aware that the building we lived in housed children and that these children never went outside. I don't know if it would have made a difference to him, but I'm pretty sure he wasn't aware that the children had HIV.

On our walk, I was also stopped twice by two separate women who gently scolded me, through sign language, for not having hats on the children even though it was an unusually warm winter day. Nine months out of the year, no respectable mother in Romania would allow her child to go out without a hat. It wouldn't be the last time I got scolded for not complying. I also had difficulty in keeping the draft out. I liked the fresh air, but the fear of the draft seemed to be a national obsession. Any breeze (warm or cold) coming through a door or window was called "current" and thought to cause anything from a cold to heart problems. My disbelief in this theory led to a continuous war of the windows at Casa Speranta. (I also fought with taxi drivers who refused to let me open the windows and breathe.)

By the time we got back to Casa, I felt that our first trip to town had been a success. It was so rewarding to see Ionel's face as he took all of life in. He especially loved seeing the horses and wagons go by. Mihaela and Costin were also excited as they pointed to the people or animals on the street, but Ionel's whole body would quiver with delight as he pointed at what he wanted me to see. Ramona and Dana-Rica were very quiet and wide-eyed for most of the trip. Ramona being quiet was unusual, so I knew this chatterbox was processing a lot. I think they were all happy to get out but also happy to be back. We all went back up to our small apartment to play and cuddle on our carpeted floor.

Nurses . . . Bobbies . . . Dallas

When we got to Post Cura #4, it was a balancing act between the Romanian staff's ways and how Starcross wanted the building to run. Post Cura #4 had been run as a hospital; we were to establish families. Under their system, the children were restrained in their cribs; we gave the children freedom and life experiences. We planned to change the building over to a family model. By example, we would set the family model and then turn it back over to the Romanians. It was never the plan to stay indefinitely. I was to be here for four months, but other volunteers would follow until a new way of treating children with HIV/AIDS had been established. This endeavor was a much larger challenge than expected; attitudes were not easy to change.

Taking down walls and changing the building's structure was simpler than changing how someone does something when their identity is involved. It was a significant change we were asking from the nurses. One of them stated it very clearly: "We had to change from nurse-centered to child-centered." Only a few of the nurses would be able to embrace this shift.

Before we introduced our new system, the staff of Post Cura #4 would arrive early, between 6:30 and 7 a.m., and get busy changing the children—all sixty of them. Changing them was not a small job since each child had to be swaddled in cloths, and there were no rubber pants or hot water; early morning could be quite the mess. Then each child was fed. If they could eat with a spoon, they did, but there was no one to teach them, so two- and three-year-olds were still only able to drink from a bottle. The menu each day was milk and formula at 7 a.m., feta cheese and water at 10 a.m., soup at noon, cheese and water at 3 p.m., soup at 6 p.m., and milk at 7 p.m. Large holes were cut in the bottles' nipples to allow the thicker soup and cheese to go through. The children were on their own to get the food in their mouths. Sometimes the holes in the nipples would be too large, and when the child would lie down in the crib, they would lose the drink. Dana-Rica, who didn't have the strength to hold the bottle, would lose much of whatever was in her bottle, leaving her hungry.

On my first day, I noticed Dana-Rica lost most of her milk in the morning. I went to the office where all the nurses congregated to smoke and talk, and not one person was with the children. I asked for more milk for Dana-Rica and was informed that this was not possible; mealtime was over. Since the nurses were on break, she would need to wait until the next feeding. At 10 a.m., the children would be changed and fed again. It was only 8 a.m. I was furious but didn't know the language or how to get the milk myself. There was only one kitchen where the food was made for the entire building. On this first day, it was more than I could negotiate. I reminded myself that this was a state-run job and, therefore, it was a guaranteed job; taking the initiative to do more than the minimum was the exception. The most important part of the job seemed to be not the children but the conversation and smoking in the break room. The break room was like a social magnet, a force that pulled the nurses in together, leaving the children alone. Dana-Rica waited. But I vowed this would be the last time.

As we changed the building from the ward to family units, a few nurses came to work with us as helpers. Dr. Matusa transferred the other nurses to another location. Thirty of the sixty children were also reassigned. The nurses that stayed were happy to work for us because we paid thirty US dollars a month, an amount double their regular pay. We called their position a "bobby," another name for a nanny. We required a lot from these women, including working long hours. But mostly, what we required was to put the children's welfare first. For some, this was not easy. One day I found one of the lower-level nurses hiding as she loaded her bag with clothes from donations to our children. She became angry when asked to put them back. She said to me, "Why should these children get these nice clothes when they are only going to die? My child doesn't have nice clothes like this." I didn't know what to say. I had learned how little most Romanians had; food and heat were a priority. I just told her to put the clothes back.

We expected the bobbies to learn our way of teaching and of disciplining a child. In Romania, when a child misbehaves, they are often spanked. Children learned by strict standards, by rote, and without movement. I saw the nurses studying for exams, and I was amazed at how they needed to memorize their material precisely as in the book, even the punctuation. Concepts did not seem to carry the same weight as the material itself. That was not to be the way of Casa Speranta. We would try to model the behavior that had been modeled for us at Starcross and was the agreed-upon treatment of children in the United States.

The bobbies were taught to redirect the children, explain and help them to learn, and, if need be, give them a time-out. This way of being with a child was taught through translation and sign language, but mostly through observation. A school based on the Montessori principles was set up, which allowed the children to direct and choose their work. Stations were set up to learn pouring, stacking, placing, and sorting, just to name a few. The kids were allowed and encouraged to move throughout the day. Of course, many of our children were too young for this type of learning. We worked with them on whatever they needed. Since each family had a mom and a bobby, each child got time. We put up small plastic mirrors so the children could see themselves. Colorful pictures from magazines were hung low to stimulate and teach the children. Toys were displayed as best we could, and the children learned to put them back. Songs and rhymes were heard in the hallways. Everywhere you looked in the building, learning was going on. The children who had been deprived for so long were being showered with words and images. All around the building, quiet lived no more; aliveness had moved in. As the children learned, the bobbies learned. We hoped that, in the future, these bobbies would become mothers for the children of Casa. This would allow us to turn the children's care back over to the Romanians, which was the intention.

The soft-spoken, very efficient eighteen-year-old Simona was the bobby for my family. Immediately, Simona picked up how we wanted the children treated. She would arrive early in the morning and share the care of the children with me. Simona loved to dress them nicely. There was such a look of contentment on her face when she dressed them just so; she reminded me of a young girl playing with dolls. Romanians don't like to be on the floor due to the national obsession with drafts. But Simona didn't mind and would spend many hours on the floor playing with the children. She helped teach my older children the necessary skills for two- and three-year-olds. Costin would find her the moment she walked in and attach himself to her hip. I liked her at once. She spoke excellent English, which she said she had learned from pop music, especially the singer George Michael. Simona and I would go on to have a long history together. To this day, I am still grateful for all the help she gave me.

Over the next couple of months, the Romanian staff and our group of volunteers had a few ups and downs, but on the whole, the children's care ran smoothly. The Romanian staff, about eight women, were doing so well that I wondered if we had prejudged them. Maybe they had been more child-centered than we realized. We saw that a couple of the nurses who had stayed on with us to become bobbies were ready to become "mothers" for their own families of five children. This worked out well because a couple of volunteers sent from Starcross had left the program early.

On the other hand, I began to wonder if I had the skills to care for so many children. Sometimes, I would lose my temper when I got tired and the kids weren't listening. I would yell and then feel really bad about it. The most challenging time for me was after Simona left for the day. I would get the children in bed and there would still be dishes in the sink, clothes to wash, toys to put away. I would need to get the children settled down by reading a book, playing soft music, or just sitting in their room and hushing them when need be. This could take thirty or forty minutes as I stared at all the work ahead of me.

After getting four out of the five children to sleep, I would need to turn all my attention to Mihaela. Mihaela always required an hour more than the other children. She just couldn't settle down. I would sit on the floor, my hand through the bars of the crib, rubbing her back, sometimes so tired I was moved to tears.

If I needed something outside of my apartment, I would go out in the hall, the common area, and see all the other Romanian moms sitting around and watching their favorite show, *Dallas*. *What am I doing wrong?* I would ask myself. *How come they can get their apartment and children settled, and I can't?* This happened every night, not just one night. The women felt sorry for me, but no one told me how they did it.

It wasn't that I was interested in watching *Dallas*. I hadn't cared to watch it when it played in the States. To this day, I don't know who shot J. R. or even who J. R. is. My problem was that I couldn't do something that seemed so simple.

One night Costin had a fever. I thought he was getting a tooth. I went to the common room to see who had some children's Advil. I knew Stephanie did, but she wasn't there. She had gone out for the evening. *I hope Mirela* [her bobby] *is watching her kids*, I thought as I went across the hall into her apartment to grab the medication off the shelf.

When I walked into the dimly lit bedroom, where the cribs, like mine, circled the room, I was confused by what I saw. Little two-year-old Georgie seemed to be caught on something. I went over to his crib to help him out and was shocked to see he had been tied by his ankle to the crib with the cloth used for diapering the children. As I looked around, I saw that all five of Stephanie's children were tied to their cribs by their ankles to keep them from climbing out while unattended, as two- and three-year-olds do. Georgie and Emile were awake and tried to stand up. I was so angry I could have screamed. *You've got to be kidding!* Is this what these women have been doing? Not these kids—not any kids, but definitely not these kids. They are not going to be treated this way, not after they had spent their whole lives trapped in a crib.

I was angry at Mirela, but it didn't take long to realize I was also angry at myself. For weeks now, I had doubted myself and my ability to mother. I had been so hard on myself when they made it look so easy. I thought, *Why do I always believe that everyone can do it better than I can?* I went out to the common area and found the TV was off, and all the women had scattered like chickens. I knew the program wasn't over, so I thought all four must be doing the same thing. It was apparent we had more to do in teaching this group what it meant to be child-centered. Once again, it felt like a balancing act: the nurses were taking care of themselves at the expense of the children, while I had been taking care of the children at my own expense. Many days I was overly tired and stressed. I would need to learn how to take care of myself better than I had. Right away, I planned to get Simona to come in to work later and leave later to help with the evening cleanup and bedtime. I felt better immediately. If I hadn't been so busy comparing myself to the Romanian moms, maybe I would have come up with this solution earlier. Meanwhile, the next day it would be back to the classroom for the moms.

Changing My Life at the Changing Table

I spent an inordinate amount of time at the changing table, changing my five children. It makes sense that this is where I worked things out in my head regarding my relationship with the children, Bill, and myself. I wanted to know where this experience was taking me; what difference it was going to make in my life. What was it going to be like for the children after I left? Who would replace me? I had only been in Romania for a little over two months, but it was hard not to think of the future.

I started early in the morning when I'd barely opened my eyes. One of the children would wake me from the adjoining room. It was usually Mihaela, who would throw open the orange and white curtain that hung on the glass partition separating our rooms. This glass wall was left over from when it was a ward so that the nurses could check on the children without having to go in. Her crib and my bed were side by side with this half-glass wall between us.

As I stumbled into the children's room, they would all be standing in their cribs, hands up, chanting

"Mama," letting me know they were ready to get out and start their day.

From my vantage point at the changing table, I could see every inch of my small apartment, from the doorway to where every child was on the floor. I could even see outside my barred windows to the yard below. The yard was just tall grass and dirt. Sometimes I saw our local friend bring his goat over to graze to keep the lawn short.

Off to the right was a huge garbage dump where our building and the apartment behind us dumped their raw garbage. Plastic bags were unheard of, so as the garbage piled up the seagulls would come in greater numbers. We could hear their loud squawks from our rooms. Each day I would look out to the gray winter sky and feel the heaviness of this country. Later in my stay, this heaviness began to feel like a ceiling of clouds holding me down, making it too hard to leave the country.

To estimate how much time I spent at the changing table, I had to think about swaddling each child. The process of swaddling involved taking two pieces of cloth; one was folded in a square, and the other was used to hold the square in place. The tricky part was flipping the child over to tie it off in the back. Changing took place at least six times a day, thirty minutes for all five kids, so three hours a day. Adding to this cumbersome process was the lack of warm water to clean them up. They would scream with the cold, and I would apologize for having to torture them in this way. Since we didn't have rubber pants, the whole process seemed futile; no sooner were they changed than they were wet again. To take the edge off of the process, I would use this time to really connect with each child individually.

I learned what each child liked and hopefully would make them feel loved. With Ramona, we might practice words that she wanted to speak so badly. Ionel was busy exploring everything and learning what each thing did. Mihaela, who was uncomfortable with a lot of physical contact, made a connection by touching pointer fingers, ET-style, with me. This simple act went so deep into my heart, but oftentimes to have this experience I would have to catch her first. Dana-Rica would laugh at just about anything, brightening my day as I laughed with her. I also used this time to do some exercises to get her body functioning. I was aware of the importance of crawling to her development, so I did cross-crawl techniques with her. After changing, she went in her bouncing chair, which got her upright and helped to strengthen her legs. Costin always needed a cuddle before he was ready to start his day.

It was during one of my many visits to the changing table that I first had the thought of trying to adopt one of the children. I had only been with them a short time, less than two months, but I already felt like I had been their mom forever. I knew adoption was a crazy thought, for so many reasons. They all were HIV positive, and the US had a law prohibiting anyone who carried the virus from entering the country. (This law stayed in effect until the end of the Obama administration.) The children were not expected to live past six years. We would have to get health insurance for a child with a terminal preexisting condition. Also, in the US, children who had two parents, no matter what the situation, were not adoptable. On the Romanian side, what had been easy was now hard. Romania now had a bad reputation on the world stage for the buying and selling of its children. There was talk that the Romanians were going to shut down any new adoptions. All of these challenges made it more or less impossible for us to adopt a child.

I'd known when I signed up for this that these children were not adoptable, so why couldn't I stop thinking about bringing one of them home? Bill would think I was crazy. As I went through the changing ritual with each one, I tried to imagine what it would be like to bring that child home with me. But every time I daydreamed about one, the others would pop into my head. Then the sobering thought that this was all just a daydream returned, reminding me that the prospect of adoption was impossible.

As I changed Ionel and then Ramona, I went through different scenarios. Here's a journal entry from that time:

> *The children's lives are getting better every day, and I am helping to make that happen. I am doing what I came to do, and that should be enough; to want more was just selfish. These children are going to be fine. They now have each other and I will see to it that they really bond with each other and learn to take care and watch out for each other. But what about*

the medical treatment I could get for them? With the right medication, maybe we can get one of the children a few more years, enough time to find a better medication or maybe even a cure.

I also told myself that I wasn't concerned about adopting a child and bonding with them, as many people were. I had recently read that research had shown that children who had been deprived of human connection for so long were not capable of bonding with another person. Although I hadn't suffered the same losses as these children, I had been adopted by and bonded with my stepmother after the death of my parents, so I convinced myself that their being adopted by me wouldn't be a problem. I made a note not to read books and articles like those unless they could offer solutions; I wasn't just going to write these children off. Then I was back to thinking about which child I would adopt. Then, in my head, a voice said, *STOP! Just STOP! This is not what you are here for.*

Hospital Stay

If I were in front of St. Peter,
I would say to him, "Let me go
to heaven because I was in hell."

—Dr. Matusa

I onel and I had not been well at all. Dr. Matusa thought Ionel had a recurrence of hepatitis B. She was unsure why I wasn't feeling well but thought some rest would help. I was so tired of not feeling well that I was willing to try. I had been listening to myself complain since I left the hospital with Tina, which was around Christmas, and now it was almost Mărțișor, the first of March.

Ionel and I were admitted to the municipal hospital. We were in the section that was delegated to infectious disease under the care of Dr. Matusa. Unfortunately, because of AIDS, Dr. Matusa's department had grown exponentially over the last year. So, after being shown to my bed, I thought the last thing that the good doctor needed was a sick volunteer to care for.

My initial impression of the hospital was the same as when I had visited a few weeks before. I felt sick at the number of children that were there with AIDS. There were seventy children, ranging in age from seven months to fifteen years. Stunned, I thought back to one of my times at the San Francisco hospital with Tina. Then, the only child there with AIDS was Tina. Now, here were so many children, sometimes more than one in a crib. And these children were so very sick. So many of them were covered in molluscum, and they also had failure to thrive and looked starved, with extended abdomens and limbs so thin they looked like they could break. Diarrhea was so prevalent that the nurses couldn't keep up. The children rocked in their beds as the nurses tried to find the room to place them all. The hospital ward was unlike any you'd see outside of a war zone or a disaster relief center.

I stayed in the wing of the hospital designated for mothers and children. That was the best and only good part of my stay. The staff was very warm, but there was a typical lack of initiative in caring for the children. I don't know, but I think the lack of focus on the children came from fear of the virus and the thought that these children were just going to die anyway. So, during the day and night, I would find the nurses knitting or socializing in the office while the children cried alone in their cribs.

The hospital was dirty. The bathroom was not cleaned during my stay, although the garbage was removed. A child vomited in the hallway, and it wasn't cleaned all night long. Cockroaches were all over the place, climbing up the wall and, yuck, across my pillow. I had a comparably private room, shared with a young woman and her blonde, curly-headed two-year-old daughter. Both of them seemed very sweet. In addition, we had a lanky twelve-year-old boy with us.

The boy had only a crib to sleep in; his legs were hanging through the bars a good two feet. One night, he handled the problem by pulling the nightstand up to put his extended legs on. He never had a visitor while I was there because his family lived far from the hospital; his mother had other children to care for. It was strange to see him taking his medication and temperature. I also administered Ionel's medication and my own. However, it still wasn't clear what was wrong with me. Every time I ate, I felt more pain. My exhaustion was constant.

Ionel and I had one bed to sleep in and stay in all day and night. When the nurses came by, they insisted that Ionel and I be in bed, which wasn't easy with a two-year-old who wanted to move. The nurses also discouraged the women in my section from gathering to share stories and information about their children's health.

Smoking was a huge part of being social in this country. Since I had smoked in the past, it wasn't hard for me to get back into it, especially when it meant I was invited to hang out with the other women on my floor. They had long, defiant talks about their medical treatment and doctors as they gathered in the stairwell to smoke. Then suddenly, someone, the lookout, would call out "doctor!" and all the women would scatter like chickens. It was such a parent/child relationship with the doctors, it made me laugh.

One night, I saw many of these same women enter the ward next to my room. I couldn't imagine what they were doing. I was surprised to see they were changing all fifteen or so children. I was unsure if this was all on the children's behalf or to help the nurses. I was invited to join in. I'm pretty sure I changed all the children that no one else wanted to touch. What an eye-opener! At Casa Speranta, I had been changing much healthier children; these children wouldn't make it too much longer. Their bodies were covered with sores. They were skin and bones, with cries so weak they could hardly be heard. They didn't have that baby smell that I loved so much. Instead, they smelled of strong urine, like an older person, even after their diapers were changed.

I was trying to wash one baby who was covered in diarrhea. There was nothing to use but a rag and cold water. The lack of care that this child was given was hard to take. I was afraid of getting too involved because this baby was so frail; I thought I might easily break the child's limbs. The conditions in the hospital were overwhelming. There was only so much of a situation that I could take in. I was learning to go somewhere else in my mind when the pain of the moment was too much. I don't know where my mind went, but when I returned, like a daydream, I knew I hadn't been present.

By the end of my third day, my roommate, twenty-one-year-old Marianna, and I had formed a bond of sisterhood. And our two-year-olds, Ionel and Katalina, were getting along equally well. This young mom was very interested in Ionel and me. She spoke a little English and wanted me to teach her more, as we sat around waiting for who knows what. We both had been there for three days, and not much seemed to be happening. We had not had any tests. We just seemed to be sitting around and waiting.

With my few Romanian words, I tried to express myself. My poor pronunciation often led to a lot of laughter. Sometimes when I wrote in my journal, Marianna would come over and read what I had written over my shoulder. For some reason, I didn't mind this. We also formed an alliance in our attitudes toward the nurses who were always telling us to get back in bed. I stood guard as Marianna sneaked off to have a cigarette in the stairwell. Ionel and Katalina were like two peas in a pod, sharing their books and toys and jumping on each other's beds. It made me think maybe after the hospital, we could all be friends.

I was coming back from the bathroom when I saw one of the doctors leaving my room. The room felt different from when I'd just left; it was quiet. The children were silent. But Marianna was crying; she had just heard that Katalina had SIDA (AIDS). She alternated between being confused and crying a deep quiet cry; her pain was cutting. Katalina was in her arms as Marianna rocked her back and forth. She was looking to me to help her understand. But I was being gagged by the language that I didn't have. I knew, or I thought I knew, that she was aware that Ionel had the virus also. Yes, I remembered she had expressed her sadness to me when we had spoken about Ionel having SIDA. Now, having learned that Katalina had it also, we had a new alliance. This one wasn't silly or fun; this one hurt.

My tears made me want to leave the room. Instead, I went over to Marianna's bed; I didn't know what to do. I spoke my words of sadness in a language she didn't understand. I smoothed the head of the child that lay in her arms. Our attention was focused on Katalina, who was peaceful, feeling our hands on her. Marianna, who was in shock, went in and out of its pain. I continued to stroke the little one's head as I was connected to Marianna and experienced her pain, witnessed her pain, acknowledged her pain.

From the corner of my eye, I saw Ionel, who had been involved with his toy, approaching the bed. I saw his little plump hand reach over and join our hands as we all soothed Katalina. Not a word was said; we stayed wrapped in silence.

* * *

Ionel and I were released from the hospital after four days. Our release took some persuading since I still wasn't feeling well, and the usual stay for Ionel with hepatitis was a week. But since there was no testing or treatment plan, I wanted to go back to Casa Speranta.

On returning home to Casa, I remembered that being with the children was the most rewarding part of being in Romania. I discovered that they were becoming my only interest and the focus of each day. I was no longer interested in what the other volunteers were fighting about or the politics of the building, or even seeing the country. The only place I wanted to be was with the kids.

While playing on the floor with Stephanie and the children, I was so relieved when Stephanie took a good look at me and said, "Your eyes are yellow." I had hepatitis A! Finally, I knew what was wrong; at last, I had a reason to lie down.

Late Teen Years/Late 1960s

B y the end of high school, my relationship with Bill was getting a bit rocky. We were on again, off again, depending on which one of us had a passing crush on someone else. But when we were together, we had a lot of fun. He still could make me laugh like no one else could. He played sports until his senior year, when his temper got the best of him, and he literally and figuratively threw the towel in. His quick temper and quick wit, which I loved so much, did not go over well with his coach.

After high school, Bill went away to college. I stayed at home and started community college. I quit after six months when my Corvair broke down. My brother Charlie had given me 350 dollars for a car when I graduated from high school. Ralph Nader later described the Corvair as unsafe at any speed. To be fair to my brother, he never really saw the car. I chose it; he just gave me the money.

My first job was at a local retail store. Then I took a job selling electric razors.

With Bill off at college upstate, I started to see other guys and often wasn't honest about it with Bill. I rented a place to live with a friend, a small cottage that was made to look like a tugboat with a deck and a stovepipe. It was funky and cool. It wasn't long, though, until I started to feel lonely. My friend spent most of her time with her boyfriend, and most nights, I was alone. Usually, I had only bread and eggs in the refrigerator, so each night, I would sit alone and eat French toast.

I was still very connected to Bill and his family. Since we first met, his parents had treated me as another daughter. When Bill's father visited me one day, he decided that my roommate and her friends were shady, hippie types; he scooped me up and got me out of the tugboat cottage, and brought me to their house to live. Without a word of protest from me, Bill's parents told me to move into his room. In hindsight, I see that they gave me what I was looking for—a home and a family. Since he was at school, Bill only came home for holidays and summer vacations. He must have liked having me there because he only sometimes complained about sleeping in the basement on a less-than-comfortable bed.

Anyway, by this time, our hormones were getting the best of us; when Bill's parents went to church, he would be at my bedroom door before they were out of the driveway.

This setup worked for us. In our nineteen-year-old minds, this way of being together was only temporary. I don't recall when we decided that we would get married. Marriage was more of a matter of course. We'd already been together for seven years. We would have loved to have lived together, but at that time, our religion and our parents' approval got in our way. Both parties spoke of couples who lived together without the sacrament of marriage as living in sin.

We should have known that we were too young to get married when we felt we needed to ask Bill's parents for permission. But we did ask, and they promptly said no, we were too young. We said we would ask again the next year, at twenty, when we were sure to be old enough. We did ask again, twice, finally getting a yes when we were twenty-one. Before we set the date for the wedding, Bill drove over to my mother's house to ask for her blessing. In anticipation of his arrival, my mother made Bill, a 175-pound twenty-year-old, a ladies' bridge club sandwich of watercress with the crust cut off. That was my mother. He wasn't thrilled with the lunch, but it served its purpose: she told him she was willing to give us a wedding.

By 1970, the US was in turmoil, with widespread protests against the very unpopular Vietnam War. Our National Guard shot and killed four students and wounded nine more at a peace rally at Kent State. The war didn't make sense to our generation; the Vietnamese didn't want us there. So why were we fighting this war? Our friends and loved ones got drafted, only to be killed or return with PTSD before it even had a name. One night when Bill was at school and I was at Ann's house, we both sat by the radio, hardly breathing as they drew lottery numbers for the draft. Bill had received a very low draft number, sixty-nine, and knew he would be called as soon as he graduated from school. Thankfully, when he went for his physical, he had high blood pressure. The stress of what was before him had given him hypertension for the only time in his life. Guys were doing some extreme things to get out of going to war. Our dear friend Walter begged Bill to drive over his foot so that Walter didn't have to go. Bill refused; Walter went to war and returned, never to be the same. My friend from work kept intentionally breaking his arm; others left the country to live in Canada. It wasn't that these young men weren't brave, but they didn't believe in the country's mission, unlike in previous wars.

The police were not respected—they were referred to as pigs—and authority figures were part of the establishment and thus looked down on. Guys who went to serve in Vietnam were accused of selling out. Ken Kesey (*One Flew Over the Cuckoo's Nest*), Tom Wolfe (*The Electric Kool-Aid Acid Test*), and Carlos Castaneda (the *Don Juan* books) were influential authors who helped usher in the era of psychedelic drugs and the hippie counterculture. Another author, political and social activist Abbie Hoffman, wrote a book called *Steal This Book*. I did. Although some of their books directly addressed the war and some didn't, these authors all spoke to not following the norm, questioning everything that the establishment put in front of you.

I once received a letter from Bill on SUNY New Paltz letterhead. He and other protesters had taken over the president's office, and he'd stolen some of the president's stationery. It was a turbulent time. Once again, the mood of the country reflected our own lives. We went to protests and concerts. The music was as passionate as our desire to do life better than our parents were doing it. Peace and love were essential, and we got a direct experience of it when we attended the historic concert at Woodstock.

We took off early in the day to attend a concert that we had been hearing about for the past month. Although we weren't married at the time and we would be spending the night, Bill's parents didn't give us any trouble about it. We took Bill's father's blue VW. I was wearing my bell-bottom embroidered blue jeans and a white cotton shirt embroidered with flowers. We both had long hair. Mine was blonde, straight, and almost to my waist. Bill had red hair down to his shoulders, much to his father's disgust. Bill had invited a friend from work to come with us. I hadn't met him before, but he seemed okay. I didn't have any idea when we met exactly how much time I would be spending with him. We headed for Woodstock, which should have been a two-hour ride. Although we think we got close to the concert, after driving in traffic most of the day and night and finally ditching the car and walking, we were never really sure we got to the concert grounds. We were in a mass of people, people walking to somewhere and from somewhere. Not hearing the best bands at that time was disappointing. But what we experienced was so much more powerful. There were masses of people, some old, some with young children, but mostly people who were the same generation as us. We were all trying to manage such a difficult situation: torrential rain; no food, water, or sleep in ankle-high mud. For at least two days and nights, we all walked and walked, with nowhere to sit or stay dry. All there was, was each other, and we peacefully cared for each other.

Peace was precisely what the young people of that time had been demanding. We wanted peace on the other side of the world; we wanted peace at home. Peace is what Bill and I and the guy in the back seat experienced during those days and nights. The experience gave us hope that if peace was possible here, among so many strangers, maybe it wasn't so far-fetched that we could create a society that lived in this way. People who were as uncomfortable and tired as I was offered me anything they had to share: food, water, dry clothing, and drugs. It didn't matter if they had been in traffic for a day or two or had walked for fifteen miles in the mud. They offered us a sign of peace without hesitation. Woodstock was so much more than a concert to us; it was an idealistic view of how we hoped to live.

Bill's First Visit

It's strange to say, but I was so much happier and felt so much better knowing I had hepatitis A. Once I received the diagnosis, I realized that it had been the fear of the unknown that had been pulling me down. I didn't know how much worse I would feel and for how much longer. Each day I woke to find I still had pain and no energy; this was so out of the norm for me. Now I knew a nonfat diet would keep me out of pain, along with ten days of bed rest; I could do this! I would be okay. Hepatitis was something I could handle. To add to my newfound attitude, Bill would be arriving shortly. Thank God.

By March 1, Romania was looking much brighter. The sun was out, and the persistent low cloud cover was gone. We had heat and hot water and, since I was sick, I had two women to help me; life looked so much cheerier. The children woke up warm (blanket sleepers from the US had arrived). Also, today was Mărțișor, a holiday celebrating the coming of spring. The word *Mărțișor*, the diminutive of *Marț*, is Romanian for "little March."

I received many brightly colored tokens from the nurses and friends I had made in my short time there.

The tokens were made from bright ribbons that sometimes had little charms or tiny flowers tied on them. Your friends would pin these tokens to your shirt and wish you "Mărțișor." The sentiment behind the gesture is similar to Valentine's Day, although this holiday seemed to be only for women; men did not receive any tokens.

The children had a great day. These last days of me not feeling well had started to wear on them. Also, they needed to get out, and today I had helpers to do that.

Bill would be on his way in just fourteen days. I began to wonder how he was going to be with the children. Would he have a favorite? Might he not be interested in the children at all?

Since being in the hospital and seeing the effects of the AIDS virus, I was much more aware of my children's fate. It was hard to believe when I looked at them that their lives were in peril. They looked so much healthier in the few months since I'd been with them. I knew that their health could change at any moment, but I wanted to believe that it would be different for them. In my dreamy, still-sick mind, I fantasized about how I could make sure they would not succumb to AIDS. Maybe if I could just give them enough love, they wouldn't get sick. I started to think about what it would be like to leave them or not leave them. What if I could bring them home with me? What a far-fetched idea that was. What were my alternatives? Staying in Romania was not an option, nor was not being with Bill.

I wasn't supposed to get out of bed, but in my excitement about seeing Bill, I found it difficult to stay put. I wanted our small apartment to look homey and nice. But every time I got going, the pain in my side reminded me that I wasn't ready to tackle much. The only thing I managed to accomplish was a large sign that said, "Welcome, Bill." Then it was back to bed to try to wait patiently for his arrival. It had been almost three months since I had seen him.

Over the past several weeks, our poor phone connection had become even more annoying. I was never able to capture for Bill what life was like in Romania. Now, in just a three-hour drive from the airport, he would understand more about the country than my words could ever say. Danny, the best driver I could find, would meet Bill. En route, they would hit potholes so deep he'd think he was taking the fast route to China. If he got out of the car, the mud would also be so deep it would be hard to hold on to his shoes. Coffee, if he could find it, would be bad, and the wagons and horses would be going so slow he'd want to scream. In addition, the constant 90-degree heat blowing in his face in the old, broken-down Dacia would make him want to ride with his head out the window. But this would never happen because Danny is Romanian and, like all Romanians, fears a draft. He would never open a window. The movement of air might give him the flu, a migraine, or even a heart problem. Bill would arrive at Casa Speranta at about 1 a.m. I thought about how he would make me laugh, telling me about his trip.

Brother Toby had a problem with Bill's visit. He didn't want Bill to stay at Casa Speranta; he would need to stay at a hotel. I found this a little strange since he was my husband of almost twenty years, but I bided my time. I didn't share this information with Bill, thinking I would work it out last minute. But since I'd gotten sick and diagnosed with hepatitis, Brother Toby had changed his mind. He decided that Bill might add some extra hands to care for the children while I wasn't feeling well. Whew! I was so happy not to have to go down that path with Bill. Since it was so late when he arrived, there was no traffic coming down the road in front of the building; I immediately heard the car as it pulled up. I ran to the door.

As we embraced, Bill pulled back and looked me over. I could tell from his expression he was concerned with how I looked. My clothes were hanging on me since I was fifteen pounds lighter than when he last saw me, and my eyes and skin were yellow. As we went up the gray concrete steps to my upstairs apartment, I saw him look around at our bare hallway and meager furnishings. I could tell he wasn't impressed. It was late, and I knew he was exhausted from his long trip. Still, I started to interpret his lackluster demeanor as not being very happy to see me. He assured me he was excited to see me and really eager to meet the children. So I immediately took him into the kids' room. Before our eyes adjusted to the room's darkness, we could hear their soft breathing, drawing us in. They were all sleeping on their backs and looked so cute in their cozy new footed blanket sleepers. Each child had a different color: Ramona in red, Ionel in yellow, Dana-Rica in blue, Mihaela in pink, and Costin in baby blue. I was so excited for Bill to meet them that I couldn't help myself, asking him, "Do you want to play with one of them?"

Occasionally waking a child up to see the full moon and brilliant stars or to attend a special event is something that I've been guilty of over the years.

Before Bill could answer, I gently rocked Ionel's crib and might have shaken him a bit until he woke up. Although Ionel was still sleepy, he was eager to get out of his crib and play with us. The three of us went into the adjoining room, our playroom, with the carpet and one comfy chair. Bill and I got down on the floor with Ionel and played with Ionel's only truck, and then Bill read him a book. I was surprised at how connected I was feeling to Bill even though we weren't discussing us, hugging, or kissing. I was aware that we were connecting through Ionel.

Bill later said, "I had never been aware of being around anyone with HIV/AIDS. I was a little bit nervous. I didn't want to get too close at first."

But that's not what I saw. I saw him on the floor playing trucks with Ionel and reading him a book as Ionel sat on his lap. The next day Bill was reading a book with Ramona on his lap, tickling Mihaela and Costin, and carrying Dana-Rica around on his back. And as the week went on, I found him kissing and hugging the children, helping them dress, and bathing them. And at night, I would find him in their room, watching them sleep, soaking up all their goodness. Even with poor health, I loved being able to share the children with Bill.

He told me later, "It was no longer you and the children; you were one, a unit."

Aside from the children, Bill was also interested in meeting Stephanie, Chuck, Sarah, and our Romanian bobbies. I loved being in the apartment with the kids, hearing Bill out in the hallway where we ate and making everyone laugh. When we were alone, I shared with him some of the difficulties I had with the other volunteers and how much of it might have come from not feeling well. He said he was amazed at how focused I was on the children and my lack of interest in the politics of the building. During his weeklong stay, he witnessed the ups and downs of our daily living.

Lately, I hadn't spent much time with the other volunteers since I had been in the hospital, then bound to my room by hepatitis, and now Bill was visiting. One by one, they had also gotten hepatitis. Our group was physically in bad shape, but through our illness, I felt much more connected with them.

In my role as a spiritual counselor, I held a service for the children on Sundays and evenings for the adults. Guess which was easier to manage, four adults or fifteen toddlers at once? The answer is fifteen toddlers. At first, gathering the children was like herding cats, but then they learned to settle down. Once they were all seated in the little room that we called the chapel—actually an old storage room with no windows—the children learned to be attentive for about three minutes, enough time to feel the quiet within themselves. This serene place was something to build on, and we did. They soon came to the chapel ready to hold hands in prayer, sing songs, and maintain the quiet for a few precious minutes. The children inspired me as they reminded me of how easy it can be to connect with one another and to our "higher self" (whatever that may mean to each of us).

The adults, on the other hand, myself included, held varied spiritual beliefs, and some of the group weren't that willing to participate in a ritual they didn't ask for. Brother Toby initiated the evening prayer without the consent of the volunteers. Our first group of volunteers (Stephanie, Chuck, and Sarah) showed only mild annoyance at having to attend, but the second group just wasn't going to have it. The volunteers came from the States as apartments were ready. From day one, the second group refused to participate. They came into the country cranky and remained that way. I don't know why, but this group of volunteers didn't end up staying long. I had the feeling that they might have had some preconceived idea about what the project was going to be like.

Even though it could be difficult, I had a few evenings with our group of volunteers that touched my soul. These evenings we would say the Lord's Prayer together, then sing "Silent Night."

Stephanie had a beautiful voice; she would sing, "Silent night, holy night, all is calm, all is bright . . . mother and child . . . sleep in heavenly peace."

I would think of the children in the building who were warm, well fed, loved, and now asleep. It was our imperfect, sickly, sometimes disgruntled group that was responsible for bringing these children, for the first time in their lives, to sleep in heavenly peace. To have such an opportunity to make a difference was a gift we all understood.

Bill attended a couple of these evening gatherings, and although we didn't speak of it, I believe he had a sense of what was being accomplished at Casa Speranta.

We had many more of those gifts coming our way in the months to come. Each accomplishment was appreciated and celebrated. In Stephanie's family, four-year-old Nicu had started to walk; at three years old, Ramona could now eat with a spoon; and two-and-a-half-year-old Dana-Rica could now stand with assistance. Other children that had been diagnosed as irrecuperable were no longer seen as such. Each time there was a significant accomplishment, we would have a party—dance, have cake (if we could find one), or do whatever we could to celebrate.

Bill was lucky enough to witness a few of these miracles during his visit. In a short time, he fell in love with my family and grew very fond of all the children in the house. Because I was still ill, we didn't get out much aside from a walk or two, but he didn't seem to have any desire to go anywhere or leave the children.

The week that Bill was with us, I never mentioned to him my thoughts about adopting; I hadn't spoken to anyone about my crazy idea. In fact, I was still trying not to talk to myself about it. Speaking about it would leave me open to questions I didn't have answers for. In addition, saying it aloud would acknowledge how much I wanted to adopt. I kept it tucked in the back of my consciousness. Then, once in a while, the thought would creep forward like a thief in the night and spread this desire. I thought I had kept my craziness from Bill that week.

So, as Bill picked up Ramona, the last child that morning and his last before he went to pack, I was incredulous to hear the words come out of my mouth. "Bill, what do you think of adopting one of the kids?" I shyly asked. *Oh no! Did I say that?* I thought as I braced for his answer.

But he didn't give me a direct answer; instead, we spoke about all the challenges that both countries presented to the adoption, like the US's ban on anyone with the virus entering the country and the requirement that all children be clearly established as orphans, abandoned by both parents. None of the children in my family met either of these qualifications; they had HIV/AIDS, and they all had two parents.

Romania was a whole other ball game since the overthrow of Ceaușescu and the realization that there were over one hundred thousand institutionalized children in the country; foreigners had come to adopt. The adoptions were being done legally and illegally. And in recent months, the country had been receiving a lot of attention worldwide for selling its children. True or untrue, there was talk of children being sold for body parts. Days into Bill's visit, Romania formed an adoption committee that immediately closed all adoptions until at least September, six months away.

As we contemplated all the challenges, it struck me that Bill wasn't acting surprised at my request; he had been thinking about adopting himself. He didn't believe I was crazy! We decided that the place to start would be to find out if we could get health insurance for a child, which Bill would check out with his company as soon as he got back to the US.

When Bill left the next day, he was a man with a mission. He was no longer just supporting me in my desire, but we were on this journey together on all levels.

The time it took him to get the answer seemed almost quicker than the plane ride back. "YES," I heard him say over the poor phone connection, "Blue Cross Blue Shield put in writing that when we adopt a child, it will be ours and covered under our policy." This news was incredible! I knew how difficult it was to get insurance in the US, especially with preexisting conditions. The first step, which we had expected to be a bureaucratic struggle, had been effortless. But what came next from Bill entirely blew me away, as it still does to this day.

He said, "But you know, Susan, we can't just adopt one; we have to go for all five. How could we ever choose?"

He voiced the words that had been my heart's desire. But I hadn't known how to say, "Can we adopt all five?"

Once again, Bill showed me the strength of his spirit and his heart, beyond anything I had ever experienced; I was moved beyond words.

I said goodbye to Bill as I exited the telephone cubby in front of Chuck's room. So many thoughts were going through my head. I now had, for the first time, the opportunity to make a conscious choice.

The voice in my head was in overdrive. *Do I want a child? Do I want a child with such an unsure future that I could/would probably lose so soon? What would be the purpose of bringing that child home? Starcross was already committed to them. Would their life be any better with me? What would this do to my relationship with Bill? Could we handle the possible loss of so many?*

I hoped I would be shown the way, that the path would be clear. I was feeling joy and confusion as thoughts swirled through my head. In my tiny room, I sat on my bed with the peaceful sound of children sleeping in the next room.

I took out my journal and made a list of the positives and negatives. The negatives: doctors, expenses, schools, too much for me to handle. . . . The negatives outnumbered the positives by more than ten to one.

In fact, the only positive I had was to love and be loved by these children. Clearly, in my mind and my heart, this was the only one that counted as I turned over and went to sleep.

Morgan Bates

Our adoption decision was profoundly overwhelming, and I needed confirmation that we were on the right path. Not too long into the process, I received word from Starcross that Morgan Bates, who owned an adoption agency called the Children of Light that dealt with Romanian adoptions, had seen the *Primetime Live* piece. She was willing to help with our adoption and at no charge. Although our Romanian adoptions would take a different direction than those through Morgan's agency, this was a positive sign. The validation was big: we were headed in the right direction.

Part II

Easter

It was Easter, and Casa Speranta was blossoming with bouquets of children. The drab, dark, uninviting building we had entered only four months ago was now in full bloom with toddlers. Anyone approaching the yard would have their eyes full of the bright yellow, blue, green, and red colors of their clothes, and their ears would fill with the joyful shrieks of our little ones as they ran around the yard. Our garbage-eating seagulls were no longer in charge; our flock of children out-squawked them. And the depressed-looking people heading toward the tram could no longer pass by and avoid looking our way. They now stopped and smiled, caught off guard by the infectious laughter of our children.

Casa Speranta was now up and running the way Brother Toby had envisioned. We had six families with five children each, one mother, and a bobby. In most cases, the children were thriving. But we always had sick children. No matter how much living we did at Casa, the threat of the virus and what it could do never left us.

We'd recently had some changes at Casa. Sarah was no longer with us. She'd been replaced as director by Marolen, who Brother Toby referred to as a gutsy Texan. Marolen was a tall blonde just turning fifty. I knew this because she spoke about her desire to dance on the table for her fiftieth birthday, and she did. Along with being the director, Marolen took a family of children; this was something that Sarah was not interested in doing and one of the reasons she and Starcross parted ways.

My children were all action and developing so fast. They had just been waiting for someone to give them a chance at life. I was constantly revising my vision for them. When I volunteered, I initially thought I was going to Romania to rock sick and dying children. What I wasn't ready for was all the living they had to do.

But as much joy as we were sharing, I had a heaviness within me; it would only be another week until my commitment to Starcross would be complete. Then, I would be heading home and leaving the children. I didn't know when or exactly how I would get back to them. I planned to go home and get all the US paperwork done. I needed to meet with the Immigration and Naturalization Service (INS) to get an exception for this adoption since the children all had two parents. This newly established law was to keep children from being bought and sold. I also needed to get an adoption agency to do a home study, and all that went with that—fingerprints, bank statements, personal and business referrals, physicals, many hours of meetings with adoption agents, and then hopefully approval. I was keenly aware that every step of the process could lead us to an insurmountable roadblock.

I was feeling so conflicted. On the one hand, I didn't want to leave the children. I wasn't even sure I could walk out the door, knowing if all didn't go well, I might never see them again. But I realized that I didn't have much of a choice. Bill and my family were in the States. It was my home. And I was tired of living in Romania with all its inconveniences. I felt closed in inside my apartment; I need openness and light.

Easter. Something about this holiday and its rituals was getting me through this time. It's hard to feel down when newness and rebirth are all around. Death is so difficult to accept when someone you love departs. But when I am in touch with the earth, underneath my sadness, there is a knowing that all is how it should be.

My children in Romania were blooming, but I had just heard from Starcross that Tina was not doing well. Sister Marti's recent call struck me harder than I had anticipated. She had said with hesitation and tears in her voice, "I am not going to come to Romania until Tina dies."

I could hear how hard this was for her to say, so final for Tina. It felt as if a weight had been placed in my heart. Words so hard to bear. Death and rebirth were all around me. The hard, dark, cold winter was retreating, replaced by sprouts of newness pushing their way to the light. The sun was warm, and flowers were starting to bloom, inspiring hope. From the day that I met

Tina, she represented hope to me in the day-to-day, hour-to-hour way she lived life. She seemed to carry a newness and a vitality for life at the same time the virus was breaking her body down. Her spirit was getting stronger as her body weakened. I had not known hope before meeting Tina. The hope that I knew was passive, and I had little use for it in my life. Hope had been about waiting for life and for the people around me to change. I remember a session with my mentor, Joseph Heller, when I was stuck on an issue and he told me, "Forget it, Susan, there is no hope." These words got me moving but with a forced hardness.

Unexpectedly, Tina was an efficient teacher when it came to hope.

She lit the way for me to look at life differently. She showed me that in adults, pain often comes from anticipation rather than from the event itself. I learned that as I saw her take on difficult medical procedures more easily than I had ever seen from an adult. She also shined a light on my fear of death as I saw her go from her illness and dying to aliveness and joy. This would happen when she would rally for a "happy" party that she might call for when least expected. This meant a dress, party shoes, singing, and clapping. She also taught me that even if your body is giving out, you still can be powerful. No matter where she was, at home or in the hospital, she was in charge. With a very royal wave of her hand, if she didn't want you to care for her, she would say, "Go." This left those who were accepted feeling very special, and everyone else feeling more rejected than if the queen herself had dismissed them.

So I learned that hope is the light in the darkness. It can be seen in the wave of a dying child or the unexpected absence of pain. It is anywhere that you look for it. It is a condition of my heart that I started to recognize. Hope gave me a newfound strength. A strength I hadn't known before. This strength was no longer about being hard or uncaring, ways I had used to protect myself in the past; it came from knowing that somewhere, in everyone, there is light.

On the evening of Marti's call, I went with Barbara, a new volunteer, to church at midnight (Easter Eve) to bring the light of Christ from the priest. Somehow this made me feel closer to Tina. This ritual consists of lighting a candle from the priest's and then carrying it home down the windy streets. It is said that you will be blessed if you get the light to your home. If you have difficulty keeping your candle lit, your behavior may need improvement. Our candle made it home, but many others didn't. When a candle loses its flame, a friendly passerby might relight it for you. I loved the symbolism in this simple gesture. To me, it spoke of how we are not perfect, but we get another chance because we are in this together.

That night, we kept a kind of vigil. As our candle burned, I sensed that Tina would not make it through the night. Again the heaviness laid in my chest. My sadness was for Julie's lost dreams, the loss of a sweet little girl I knew, and a reminder of the loss that was yet to come. How many more children would we lose to this disease? It made me wonder why I wanted to enter into this with so many children.

Tina died the following day.

We knew before we received the call; our candle had gone out. I wanted to call Julie to connect with her. She and Tina had made such an impression on my life, and I wanted to let her know. Stephanie beautifully said, "More than anything else, Julie and Tina are our model of what we hold dear as we care for our children."

She was such a sweet, beautiful girl. To have known Tina was a gift I treasure and will never lose.

From Woodstock to Wall Street, 1970s

B ill and I got married in 1971, and my brother, Charlie, got him a job on Wall Street. From Woodstock
to Wall Street—this job, along with getting married,
was seen by many of our friends as the ultimate sellout.
Marriage was viewed as just another institution to be
defied. At his new job, Bill stayed in New York City mul-
tiple nights a week, entertaining customers. I needed
help understanding or appreciating his strategy of
wining and dining customers to get their business. I
thought his business relationships should be based on
performance, not on who spent the most money. But
that was Wall Street at the time. And for me, it was a lot
to take in. The money came fast, too fast. I fought it—
at least, I thought I did. Bill seemed to embrace it. My
stepmother had taught me to value money; it was not
to be wasted. It was to be used sparingly only on things
she considered of value.

Bill was wasteful with his money, spending it on
new cars, clothes, expensive dinners, and concerts.
I saw these expenditures as throwing away money,

especially when he drank, which was often a problem. He bought me jewelry and a mink coat, and I put them aside, too embarrassed to wear them.

I remember the Christmas he gave me the mink coat. We were opening gifts at his parents' house, and I thought to myself, *Did I say I wanted this? It's not me—or is it? Is this who I am now?* I had the flu, so my disappointing lack of excitement wasn't taken too seriously. But I did have many questions going around in my head. Did I give Bill the wrong message? Did he buy it to impress me, our friends, or his colleagues? I was definitely at odds with it all; I didn't enjoy it when Bill expressed his love for me with money. He was feeling his love rejected.

In later years, I came to understand Bill's relationship with money. He was in a business whose only product was money. He traded corporate bonds and never saw a bond his whole time on Wall Street. The value he placed on himself was based on how much money he made. There was only one other gauge for his performance: honesty. Bill was known by his colleagues for being upstanding. He was steadfast in how he approached a job that offered many opportunities to take advantage of the system. His beliefs about correctness in business led the guys at one shop he worked at to mock him by calling him "choir boy." This nickname was a jab, not a compliment, but I loved this about him. It made me proud that he was thought of in this way.

As Bill was finding his way on Wall Street, I was learning about who I was and wasn't. During the first couple of years of our marriage, we lived in an apartment complex building built up to an embankment. When I looked out the windows, all I saw were boulders and dirt. The apartment was cold and dark. I didn't care for my retail job and knew no one in the area. While Bill was starting his exciting new job, I was getting increasingly lonely and depressed. Night after night, I was alone at home, as Bill was doing what was expected of him: entertaining customers, developing relationships. I didn't handle being alone well, and with little self-awareness, I flirted with other men. I always knew of some guy I thought would be interested in me if I lost Bill. I, unknowingly, had a backup plan; I wasn't going to take a chance on just one person again. What if something happened to Bill or he left me for someone else? These flirtations mostly kept me from feeling lonely, but one led to a brief affair that Bill learned of. When he confronted me, I saw the pain of betrayal in his eyes; I couldn't bear it. I tried to justify my actions by making him wrong. He was never home, he drank too much, whatever else I could think of, as long as I didn't need to see or feel his cutting pain. For many years this event was like a monkey on my back; it never seemed to go away. Although, after the initial blow-up, we rarely spoke of it, we both knew it was there, like a special weapon that could be pulled out at any time. And I carried the knowledge that I wasn't a contender, as Bill was, for any honesty awards.

After a few years, we moved from the darkness into a well-lit apartment in Princeton, New Jersey. I worked for two brothers who owned the first discount designer shopping mall in the state. They were very successful. I worked first as a store manager, then as an area manager, and finally as a buyer. I loved working for the Seaman brothers. They both had a great sense of humor and instinctual ability in business. I returned to school in the evenings to learn what I needed to succeed in this business. Although the brothers ended up selling their stores, I stayed on and worked for the new company.

Between Bill's job, my job, and school, Bill and I saw very little of each other, although we did commute daily by train to New York City. Since it was early morning, we weren't at our best and usually fought. It seems like a joke, but we often fought about who got what section from the *New York Times*. Bill thought I should be unquestionably happy with the Metropolitan Report, while he took over the balance of the paper. Our fighting would start then and often carry into the night. It never occurred to us to buy two papers; the paper just represented our discontent with each other and our marriage.

We both wore suits. He was comfortable in his; I was not in mine. Suits, high heels, and briefcases were as uncomfortable as the job, which required me to buy sportswear for a large chain of stores. I stayed until the new boss recognized that the job didn't fit me. When I wasn't comfortable, I didn't assert myself or do business the way my boss wanted me to. The day he fired me, as I stood before his desk, he said, "Susan, you don't belong in this business. I am going to do you a favor and let you go. You may not appreciate it now, but in the future, you'll see that I was right." He was.

One of the Seaman brothers was interested in a new movement called holistic health and the new age movement. He introduced me to a holistic chiropractor, nutritionist, astrologist, and acupuncturist, and to Erhard Seminar Training (EST), a kind of therapeutic personal transformation program, among other things. He was passionate about everything that he did. And since I wasn't happy with my job or marriage, I tried many of the experiences he suggested. Some of it seemed weird, and some changed my attitude and understanding of life. For example, EST was one of the experiences that changed my perspective on being responsible. I learned that I alone was responsible for my life. I could no longer blame anyone or any circumstances for my life not being how I wanted it to be. Instead, I learned to choose to be deeply responsible. This shift in attitude was not always easy to accept, but when I did accept this way of thinking, I felt more powerful and in control of my life.

This was the seventies. It was the time of Watergate, the end of the Vietnam War, women's lib, gay rights, free love, disco, and *Roe v. Wade*. I started defining myself by establishing who I wasn't more than who I was. I supported women's lib by ensuring I didn't fall into a woman's traditional role in a marriage. I wouldn't be the one who did all the dishes, cooking, or cleaning; Bill would do his part even though men didn't do any of that in his family home.

After I left my position as a buyer, I spent the next couple of years deciding what I wanted to do with my life. I went back to school and studied art history, thinking I needed a degree. Also, I had an interest in art and antique appraisal. Along with school, I renewed the meditation practice I had started when we married. We had received a Transcendental Meditation course as a wedding gift. I loved the quiet feeling I achieved through my practice.

My life was pretty laid back; I was relaxed. We had been trying to have children, but that wasn't happening. We must have started trying in the late seventies because I remember getting off the train from New York City, rushing home to have sex, and then running to the doctor's office for a test. The whole process felt forced. We had attended meetings at adoption agencies that left us feeling the same way—forced, not natural. We wanted a child, but it was hard to get excited when it was just paperwork and waiting for years. So our attitude was, if it happens, it happens; we weren't going to do anything more about it. In hindsight, I think we were both afraid to put so much effort into something we weren't sure we could accomplish.

I was sitting at the small round table in our townhouse kitchen in Yardley, Pennsylvania, drinking a morning cup of coffee. I had just dropped Bill off at the train station. I was leafing through a magazine I had picked up at the Holistic Health Association of Princeton's charter meeting the night before. The more I learned about this new way of thinking about health, the more sense it made. I was introduced to the mind/ body connection and being responsible for my well-being. I learned that the answer to illness need not always come from a bottle. Moreover, I became proactive regarding my body; I no longer waited for pain to take care of it. I started to exercise.

As I turned the magazine page, I went back, unsure about what I had read. There was a small ad on the page before me. I recall the side view of a man's skeleton walking in the ad box. There were bullet points down the ad's side:

- *work independently*
- *create your hours*
- *make 30,000 plus a year*

The work was called Hellerwork. As I looked at it further, it seemed similar to chiropractic. Now, this was of interest.

I immediately called the number on the ad, wondering where I was calling. Cindy from Mill Valley, California, picked up the phone. I could tell by how she spoke she had also done the EST program. A large part of EST was about linguistics and being clear about your communication. She told me no one was doing Hellerwork on the East Coast, but she thought a practitioner was coming to visit, and I could try the work then. If I liked it, the training was fifteen hundred hours done in three phases: two weeks of residency in California, twelve weeks of independent study at home, and six weeks back in California. I didn't think Bill would be crazy about this and the time away from him, but I was very interested.

In a few weeks, I went to New York City to get a session. I had never had anything like this done to me before. I had never even had a massage; this was much deeper work. I had a woman practitioner who spoke with me about alignment, breathing, and balance. I can't say that I felt much different after the session than I did before. My body awareness at that time was nonexistent. My body's purpose was to carry my head around. But as I came out onto the sidewalk of Ninth Avenue, I immediately went to the corner and picked up the pay phone to call Bill.

When he answered, he asked, "How was your session?"

"It was okay." I tried to sound enthusiastic. "I'm going to go to California to sit before a selection committee. I want to train to do this work." I told him about the time commitment and the cost of the training. From the tone of his voice, I was now very sure he didn't like the idea.

Still, he didn't tell me not to go. I felt like I needed this experience to learn something new on my own, to stretch my wings. This new direction was the first time I was consciously aware of being driven or guided to do something that seemingly came to me out of nowhere. I felt an unquestionable desire to follow this knowing and trusted it.

Sister Julie and Tina at Starcross

A last goodbye, Ionel and his Romanian mom

The first day the children were put in Susan's care
(left to right: Ionel, Loredana [Dana-Rica], Costin, Mihaela, and Ramona)

Left: A voodoo solution for getting your man back. Right: Susan waits to greet Bill for his first visit to Romania.

Bedtime in the US (left to right: Ionel, 3;
Mihaela, 3; Ramona, 4; and Loredana, 3)

One big family (left to right: Aidan, 18 months;
Loredana, 8; Ramona, 9; Ionel, 8; and Mihaela, 8)

Hellerwork

I t was 1982 and I was thirty-two when I started this new adventure. After being accepted to the program, I returned to California a couple of months later to begin my first residency program. It was at Westerbeck Ranch in Sonoma. The ranch was everything you might think of when you imagine Sonoma, California. It was a small resort hidden from the road by lush trees and plants. There was a big redwood barrel hot tub, big enough for ten people; a pool; and a round wooden group building. The round building was where we had class every day. It could accommodate twenty students, teachers, work tables, and movement lessons. This was where we would spend twelve hours every day for fourteen days.

I loved every moment of my training. I loved learning about our bodies and how they were meant to move, alignment, anatomy, and the body's knowledge.

Joseph Heller, the founder of Hellerwork, and his work greatly influenced me. He had been an aerospace engineer with NASA prior to his work with Ida Rolf and extensively trained with some of the leading figures in the humanistic/health movement.

With such a diverse background, Joseph brought an understanding of the mechanical, energetic, and emotional complexities of the body. He taught me to see misalignments in the body and how each affects the whole structure. He also educated me about movement and emotional awareness to support the body's alignment. I learned that the body has an integrity of its own. I started to trust and learn from my body, an experience I had never had before.

As I witnessed his work with clients, somewhere over forty hours, I saw this regular guy time and time again enter into a session in such a nonjudgmental way, with such love and compassion, that his clients often would heal by this alone. This way of being is how he did his sessions and taught his classes. Through his open-hearted teaching, I learned like never before. I not only learned the work but owned it for myself. From Joseph Heller, I learned how to enter into this healing space myself, which I believe made me almost immediately successful with my own practice.

After my initial two weeks of residency, I did a home study for twelve weeks. When my twelve weeks were up, I returned to Sonoma for several more weeks of residency training. During this time of learning and living in a healthy environment, I experienced feeling creative, happy, and free. Free to be me.

I had a new friend, Jackie, who embodied this new spirit I desired. I also made new male friends. I could tell from our phone conversations that these relationships were not sitting well with Bill. He was feeling jealous and resentful. He wanted me home. So when the time came to end my training and return home, I was sad to go but also feeling excited to see Bill and start my new business.

Bill picked me up at the airport. Before I had a chance to give him my plan for my business, he told me his company had offered him a transfer to London. In my new open "let's go for it" state of mind, I answered by quoting Helen Keller, "Life is either a great adventure or nothing." I would soon regret those words.

Return to the US, May 1991

I can hear Dana-Rica's angry cry coming from down the hall. It's early in the morning, and the kids are just waking up. I can't see her, but I know that she's on the changing table, one of our favorite places to connect. She is looking for me and isn't happy that I'm not there. I am now sleeping down the hall. This transition was supposed to make it easier for the children. Cristina, our new volunteer, and I decided that I would move to a bedroom down the hall to prepare the children for my departure. This arrangement is supposed to allow me to separate from the kids a bit and yet still stop in and spend time with them, thereby making it easier for all. But it may not be working that well. Last night, Ionel wouldn't kiss me goodnight after I hadn't been with him most of the day. Cristina told me he had been acting out by being mean to the other children. Now, hearing Dana-Rica's screaming, it doesn't sound like it is working for them; it certainly isn't working for me.

Like Dana-Rica, I, too, have spent half my days crying. The time has come for me to leave the children and return to the US. This is the end of my six-month commitment to the program. It is also the beginning of our quest to adopt the children. We will need to get permission from the State Department and get a home study done. I hope to return to Romania to pick up the kids as quickly as possible. The thought of returning is the only thing keeping me from severe depression and crying all day instead of half. It is pit-of-my-stomach painful; it feels as if I am losing them. What if I can't get back to them if we can't pull off this adoption?

Cristina, a preschool teacher from Colorado, couldn't be a better replacement for me. But Dana-Rica is a determined girl, and I can tell that her crying has now moved to a new level of anger. Anger because I am not coming. After all, I have been hers, her mother. I am the only person she, at almost three, has ever had of her own, and she wanted me there just like I had been for these four last months. It was killing me not to go to her.

MAY 1, 1991, JOURNAL

Well, the day is finally here; I'm leaving tomorrow. I am writing from my room in Bucharest. This morning I got to spend some time with the children before I had to go. I felt kind of shut off from them, too drained to allow myself to cry and feel the pain of leaving them. I kissed each of them goodbye, knowing that they couldn't understand that I was planning on returning to them. It will be just another loss for them. Leaving them upstairs, I gathered my bags and hurried downstairs and out the door. At first, I thought I heard their voices in my head, "Mama, Mama," but as I turned and looked up, I suw them out on the balcony. Their little heads were just making it over the railing as they waved good-bye and called my name. I tried to look happy, but I could hardly look at them. There has been too much leaving going on in my life, with Bill and now leaving the children. When I finally get them all together, there will be no more leaving for a very long time!

* * *

I was all settled in my hotel room in Bucharest. My flight was to depart the next day. I wished I could have gone directly to the airport, but the three-hour ride from Constanta to Bucharest made it impossible to catch an early morning flight. Even though it was May and the weather was warm, there was a chill in the room. The decor was heavy-looking, with reddish brushed-velvet drapes. I found the place depressing from the moment I walked into the hotel, passing the typical four or so shady-looking men dressed in black who were probably trying to change money on the black market. I was in the midst of sorting through my bags for something to read in English when there was a knock on my door. Probably too quickly, and without asking who was there, I opened the door. Thankfully, it was Luca, Dr. Matusa's assistant. She wanted me to go to the US embassy with her to get her visa. She planned on going to Newark, New Jersey, to the pediatric AIDS clinic to study. Luca was a twenty-something who was extremely direct and efficient with her words. She started her conversation with me when she was barely in the door of my room, her coat still on.

"Susan," she said, "Why do you want to adopt these children? I would like to know, and so does my husband. Why not adopt a healthy child?"

I told her, "It wasn't a healthy child that I fell in love with. It was my five children."

Then she hit me over the head with her very blunt words, "You know they are going to die, and what if you find that you have made a mistake?"

Feeling annoyed, I said, "What choice would I have? What choice does any mother have? You have to go on. And how could loving a child ever be a mistake?"

I was about to tell her I was tired and needed to sleep so that she would leave when she told me that she was four months pregnant. I then understood the questioning and also why she asked on behalf of her husband. I also understood that this might be the first of many hard conversations to come with people who just couldn't understand.

I was finally on my way home after spending three days in Bucharest waiting for a flight; one after another had been canceled. Since I never did find anything to read in English, I spent the last days roaming the streets of Romania's capital. In the thirties, Bucharest was known as "little Paris." I could see traces of that as I walked the city. Some of the architecture still remains, and the city has its smaller version of the Arc de Triomphe. But Bucharest has gone through a lot—the war, two earthquakes, and Ceaușescu—and it shows. Ceaușescu was responsible for taking down many beautiful homes and buildings to make way for

Soviet blocks and his massive palace. In some areas of the city, street children can be seen everywhere, begging, stealing, and doing what they need to stay alive. In other parts of the city, I was warned not to travel down certain streets because packs of dogs would attack.

So I was happy to be saying so long to this land of inconveniences. On the whole, Romania did not feel dangerous to me, but it lacked almost any conveniences. Just getting to the airport, I'd faced no hot water in the hotel and no light in its pitch-black hallways, a broken elevator (so I'd had to climb seven flights of stairs with two huge bags in the dark), and of course, the obligatory fight with the taxi driver, who overcharged me.

The day got more difficult for me when I entered the airport terminal. At first, I noticed how many babies I was passing on my way to the gate. But, as I approached my gate, I was shocked by what I saw. More babies! Six weeks, five weeks, two weeks old—all being held by their new American parents. I'd experienced some of this phenomenon a few days before when I visited the US embassy with Luca. There were many babies with couples who were trying to work the system to adopt them. But today was incredible! It looked like a baby sale at Macy's before Christmas. I could see the infants on the display table with a sale sign that read "BABIES! GREAT PRICE! GET THEM WHILE THEY'RE LITTLE!" It felt like a baby market. It isn't easy to adopt an infant in the US, at least not one that may look like you. Romania's problem had offered a new resource for children. Since the overthrow of Ceaușescu, seven thousand Romanian children had been adopted, and more than fourteen hundred had gone to Americans.[*]

I was like a bottle ready to pop. Angry? Sad? Was I mad because I thought this wasn't right? I didn't know each couple's situation, so who was I to judge? Or was I sad and angry because I resented them? Because they had what I wanted? Maybe a little of both. I did know that this was the reason Romania was closing down its adoptions. The government had gotten bad publicity over children being sold. Of course, this wasn't the majority of adoptions, but a small and profitable market in children had diminished Romania in the eyes of the world community.

My thoughts returned to my children and to what Luca had said. I didn't know why, but I wasn't interested in pursuing a healthy child; it didn't feel right. I know that had I been involved in adopting another child during this time, I couldn't have given my children what they needed.

I overheard a conversation as I was waiting to hear my flight called. It was between a thrilled new mom with a baby (I wasn't sure of the baby's age; I didn't want to turn around) and an older Romanian woman.

---

[*] David Binder, "U.S. Issues Warning of Obstacles in Adopting Romanian Children," *New York Times*, May 24, 1991, *https:// www.nytimes.com/1991/05/24/world/us-issues-warning-of -obstacles-in-adopting-romanian-children.html.*

The older woman spoke excellent English. As she spoke, I sensed that she was hurt and embarrassed by her country's inability to care for its children. I got teary thinking of the country's collective pain from having to give up its most special gift: its children.

As I watched the new parents try to figure out their new family members, my thoughts went back yet again to Luca and what she had said to me. Was I taking on too much? Yes, probably. I was opening myself up to so much sickness and death. But, much to my surprise, it didn't seem to be an issue. As I got up to board the plane, I quickly put out my plea to the universe. *Please show me the way.*

Stuck, May–August, Princeton

Stuck, trapped, and unable to move. This pretty much sums up the months I spent back in Princeton as I waited for the adoption proceedings to advance. No matter what I did, I couldn't gain any ground on the adoption nor get back to my previous work and life; I was in limbo.

Before I left for Romania, I had put my practice of structural bodywork on hold. I told my clients I would return in six months to resume work. I had referred them to other practitioners in the area. Now that I had returned, I was torn about how much effort to put into reconnecting with these clients, knowing that I might be leaving again. This wouldn't be fair to them.

Now, for the first time since I'd started my practice, I lacked clients. I also had a business partner. We ran yearlong Hellerwork training, which was a lot of work since seven weeks of the training were residential. This meant feeding and housing students and faculty. My partner was expecting me to jump in and get our next program enrolled. There was too much for one person to handle. That summer, I just couldn't get the program off the ground. I could hear my partner's disappointment as we realized we just didn't have the number of students we needed to put on this year's training.

To say I was happy to be home isn't quite accurate. I was happy to be with Bill, certainly. I was also happy to be with my friends again, even though these visits sometimes felt awkward. I learned that my experience over the past several months in Romania was mine, and mine alone. Despite my friends' caring, it felt like they couldn't truly understand my experience. They didn't know what it felt like to have a child's arms pulling against my neck as I tried to put him down. Or the pain that I saw on Julie's face when she couldn't do any more for Tina. I wasn't able to transport them to the thrill of seeing Nicu walk. Or have them feel the pain in my ribs from laughing so hard the day the children, led by my little nymph Mihaela, had covered the apartment and themselves in baby powder. How could they ever know it? I could only bring them words.

My return to the US was also filled with mixed feelings about my relationship with our country. On the one hand, I had missed the efficiency of the good old US. We get things done! It was so different from Romania, where whatever was asked, the answer always seemed to be the same: "Not possible." In the US, we really do grow up believing anything is possible. It was with that invincible attitude that we were moving forward to adopt the "unadoptable" children.

But what I witnessed in the US that I could not unsee was our massive amounts of everything. If inequality were a mountain, we would be king of it. With new eyes, I felt so wrong belonging to a country that had so much more than most of the world, only to want more. In Romania, if you wanted a soda, you could choose between Coke and Orange. Here there is a whole aisle in the market devoted just to soda. There are ten different kinds of milk. Shampoos, again, have a whole aisle of choices. This was not new information for me, but it felt so wrong, so excessive. It also bothered me how wasteful we are with food in restaurants and at home—all the excess that was thrown away. I saw how much paper and plastic we waste because everything we buy is wrapped and wrapped again.

But I had no idea what to do with all these feelings; they just hung over me like a dark veil dimming my enthusiasm about being home.

Although these problems were shadowing me, the country was experiencing a high that summer. We felt victorious, having won Desert Storm. Our troops were coming home. I attended the ticker tape parade down the Canyon of Heroes in Manhattan. It would have been hard not to get pulled into the patriotism that was in the air that day. George Bush was so popular that it would have been difficult to believe he would be a one-term president.

* * *

The first call I made in regard to the adoption was to an agency to set up our home study. This project was not as easy as I had thought. My first call to an international agency did not go well. The response I got from the snarky social worker was, "Five children? Why don't you take ten or twelve?"

Not to be put off, after a few more calls like that, I finally found a local agency to do the work.

Starting our home study was a bit like putting the cart before the horse since, to go any further with the adoption, we needed the approval of INS. I had submitted our application, but we knew it might take a while. So Bill and I took a chance and moved ahead with the home study even though we knew if our case were denied, our time and money would have been spent for nothing. We were equally committed to adopting the children, so it seemed that whatever we had to do, we would.

We felt closer and more connected all the time. There were many meetings that went into the home study. Plus, we needed physicals, fingerprints, police records, character recommendations, and financial records. Of course, each child was a separate adoption, so the amount of paperwork involved was starting to pile up. As we did this work, the *New York Times* and other publications printed articles such as "U.S. Issues Warning of Obstacles in Adopting Romanian Children," describing how difficult it had become to adopt from Romania.

All through May, June, and July, we waited. I had engaged a Romanian lawyer and spoken to him a couple of times. He let me know that even though adoptions were closed in Romania, he could file our case with the court, and we could move ahead as soon as we got permission from INS. So we waited.

During this waiting period, a strange thing happened to me. I got a bite on my stomach from a tick. At first, it was just an irritated bite, but as the days went on, it got more and more painful. My stomach blew up like I was pregnant. The pain was piercing; it hurt in any direction that I moved. Because of the pain, I started to get out of a chair and walk the way a pregnant woman might. I'm not someone who gets to the doctor easily or quickly. I didn't even have a regular doctor at that time. So when I finally went, not a moment too soon, I discovered that I needed to be hospitalized for an internal abscess. They operated on me immediately, and I was given several antibiotics to kill the sixteen different kinds of bacteria that had come from the tick. My hospital stay lasted a week. Then, for the next month, I was treated at home with IV antibiotics, which really limited my activities and what I was able to do.

After the pain was gone, it struck me how serendipitous it was that I was trying to have children, and my stomach blew up. I had months of waiting, restricted movement, pain, and a hospital stay. All that was missing were the kids.

I was moody. I felt like a pregnant woman in her ninth month who had just had enough of the discomfort and the endless wait.

Bill was extremely patient and gave me a lot of space. He was just so happy to have me home. He treated me like a queen or a guest in the house. He was so nice I started to feel bad about being so grouchy, but I didn't seem able to stop myself. Sometimes I wished that he would react with the anger that I deserved.

It was early one Saturday morning, and I was making coffee in the kitchen. The sun was out, pouring into the kitchen through our huge glass window. The window had needed to be specially ordered because I can never get enough light. But this day, even the sun wasn't cheering me up. I'd had enough of being in limbo, neither here nor there. Although my back was turned to Bill, I could feel him kind of sneaking by as he headed out to the dentist. My words caught him as he was almost out the door.

"Bill, we need to make plans about what we're going to do."

He seemed to know exactly what I was talking about. So I continued, "I need to get on with my life. I can't live like this; nothing's happening. I can't go back to my old life, and this adoption is going nowhere."

He shot back, "It sounds like you're giving up," and headed out the door.

Now I was left with myself and my own discontent. As the sun continued to warm the room but not my mood, I sat at the kitchen counter to finish my coffee. All of a sudden, there was a car horn beeping. It sounded like it was coming down the driveway.

Bill was back. He popped through the kitchen door with such excitement. "Susan!" he exclaimed. "I was headed down the road and I just had a feeling I should go back and check the mailbox, that there was an answer for us. So I backed the car all the way down the road to check. And there it was!"

INS had approved our first application. We could move ahead.

"Wow!" we said in unison as we hugged.

We knew this was good, a first step. This was movement. This was what we had been waiting for.

My thoughts went to the day that I had driven to the INS office in Newark to apply for the adoption. I had waited the obligatory hour before being called back to review my application. How lucky, how blessed, was I that the woman who sat behind the gray metal desk seemed to care what I had to say. These children did not qualify for a US adoption. There was a law that stated the child being considered for adoption could not have two parents in their country of origin. In fact, this law was posted all over the office. All of my children had two parents. She clearly had the law on her side to dismiss the case right there and then, but she didn't. She took the application, said they would be in touch, and wished me luck. It was this one woman who was willing to treat me with such humanity, not just as a form, who made such a difference in so many lives.

On Monday, I spoke with the Romanian lawyer, Bese Sorin. He said he would check with the court to see how they were going to view the case. He would let me know on Thursday.

Now, for the first time, when I called Casa Speranta, I asked to speak with the children. I could do it now. Now there was hope. Hope? Had I forgotten what

I had learned? Had I forgotten to look for the light in the darkness? I quickly decided I had. I noted the lesson learned. All the signs had been there: feeling lost, depressed, and the familiar hardness to my life. Now there was a good chance I would be going back. I opened my heart, allowed myself to know how much I missed the children, and renewed my sense of hope that we would be together soon.

Lessons to Be Learned, 1983

My regret kicked in after I realized that Bill being transferred to London meant I would also have to go. It wasn't that I didn't want to live in London, but I had just opened up my practice in Princeton, and I was doing very well. I was also working in New York City and loved working there with dancers. The work was new to the area, and people were interested. But we had rented out our house, and it was just a matter of time before I would need to join Bill in London. For a few months, from August through November, I tried to travel between Princeton, New York, and London, working in all locations and staying with friends, but it was tiring and not very practical. Bill had already moved to London, and I had been dragging my feet getting there for four months. And although I was ignoring it, Bill was getting angry with me. He didn't like the people that I was hanging around. We would fight about what I was doing and with whom. He said he was lonely and unhappy, but I was so excited about what I was doing that I didn't hear him. Finally, it began to dawn on me that for my marriage, I needed to be in London.

As the plane landed at Heathrow, I was looking forward to seeing Bill. Our time apart made me realize how much I loved him. I felt my resentment about needing to give up my new business fading away. I was almost feeling good about staying in one place. Listening to "Islands in the Stream" playing from my headset, I continued to think about how much I had missed being with Bill. I put on lip gloss and brushed my hair. He was right there as I came through customs and looked so good. But I quickly sensed a coolness about him. I thought, *I guess we have a few things to work out.*

As soon as we got to the car, he turned to me and asked angrily, "Why are you here?"

"What do you mean, why am I here? I'm here to be with you. I gave up my new practice to be with you," I said, meeting his anger.

"Well, I don't want you here anymore," he said in a manner I had never heard from him before.

I was in disbelief and shock as my stomach turned. "Aren't we going to talk about this?" I asked with tears in my voice.

He reluctantly agreed. But that week, we barely talked unless we were fighting. Each of us was accusing the other of being responsible for getting us to this place. We concluded the week by seeing a marriage therapist.

Now that I was finally resolved about giving up my new practice in New York and Princeton and living in London, I was fighting for our marriage.

But Bill was no longer interested, and I wasn't exactly sure why. When he finally agreed to see a therapist, it was with the agreement that we only spoke about how we would separate; he still very much wanted me to leave. I decided to do it his way since it seemed to be my only choice.

As we sat at opposite ends of the therapist's plush gray couch, mirroring the ocean that had separated us both physically and emotionally, Bill said to the lovely English woman who sat across from us, legs crossed at her ankles and hands folded on her lap, "This will be my only time here. I want to separate."

Looking lost in her overstuffed chair, the therapist asked in her soft-spoken voice about our history together.

"How did you two meet?"

"What attracted you to each other?"

"Describe your connection with each other's families."

None of these questions sat well with either of us. They hurt to answer. The therapist was right. We had shared so much together; there were many memories. It seemed like she was trying to rekindle our feelings for each other. She sensed our discomfort and sadly looked from me to Bill and back again; then, to our utter dismay, she got tears in her eyes. Bill and I looked at each other. I felt connected to him for a brief moment in our shared disbelief. I thought he was thinking what I was: *What do we do now? Do we hand her a tissue and tell her it will be all right? Or do we hug her?* She continued talking to us about the strength of our shared history. Since I wanted to stay together, I wanted her to go on, but Bill wanted no part of this discussion. Finally, he conceded to speaking with her privately, and I was asked to leave the room. When I rejoined them, he was even more resolved about separating. I was starting to sense that there was more going on than I was aware of. So we left the crying therapist's office, with her words and her reaction about our history clinging to me.

There were two things I didn't know at the time. First, as a therapist, she needed to be quite sure of herself to do what she did; she mirrored our sadness back to us. Sadness we had not acknowledged. A sadness so deep that the thought of going into it felt like falling into a black hole, never to return. I also didn't know but soon learned—after my prodding, yelling, and crying—that Bill, in his loneliness, had found someone else.

So I returned to Princeton. Our separation was the most painful experience I have ever had. The pain was unbearable. It brought up feelings of being alone and abandoned. This possible loss of my soulmate triggered memories of losing my parents, which I had done so well in avoiding, unacknowledged, in my heart and mind. Although I wanted my freedom, I also wanted to know that Bill was there. My tears never stopped.

As with the therapist, Bill's family and our friends were very upset by the thought of us divorcing. Each time I saw a friend of ours, I could barely speak, fighting back the tears and the sadness of my loss. Each time

I told our friends or family, I felt their sense of loss, also. Bill and I had been together for so long. Bill and Sue had been something they could count on. Their loss was as real as mine.

I heard that Bill had brought Devin, his new, blonde girlfriend, with him on a visit to New York and to dinner at his parents' house. It seemed that his relationship with her was getting serious. I knew Devin from a party I had attended in London. I had found her to be nice enough. When she and Bill became involved, she said she was going to fight for him, and she did. I also heard through the grapevine that Devin said that Bill treated her like a princess. To be treated like a princess was precisely what I *hadn't* wanted. I had rejected that treatment; it made me feel weak. Finally, it dawned on me that caring for someone made Bill feel good. I started to contemplate whether I could do "princess." I laughed with friends about it. Through the laughter, I came to understand what Bill had needed and realized there could be worse things to compromise on.

After nine months, Bill was transferred back to the US. We were in contact with each other but not getting along. His girlfriend was still in London and was planning on coming to the States.

Bill and I decided it was time to move things along, so we arranged to meet with a mediator. We didn't want any more fighting; we wanted an amicable divorce. We walked into a very bland office set in an office complex, ready to go. Each of us was thinking about how we would settle our financial affairs. As we spoke to the mediator, who looked like a friendly neighbor, I realized that Bill wanted me to be taken care of financially. I appreciated his gesture. I must have gotten a little teary because all of a sudden, the lawyer said from behind his desk, "I am going to leave you two alone for a while to talk things through." I don't remember what we said to each other while he was out of the room. When he returned, he asked us a few more questions. Then he said, "I want you two to go home and think about this. You two aren't ready." He didn't say why, but he had just fired us.

Getting a divorce was harder than we thought. We had brought the therapist to tears, friends and family were giving us a hard time, and our lawyer had fired us. It felt like we were pushing a boulder up a mountain. It had almost been a year, and we weren't making any progress. It was time for magic, black magic.

Over the past year, I had gone on vacation to Guadeloupe with my girlfriend Jackie. During our time there, I was still in the dumps about Bill. Although I did meet a man on this trip that I liked and dated for the next few months, in my heart, I was still very involved with Bill. So, to cheer me up, Jackie, who had long blonde hair and was extremely impish, took me to the market. She whispered something about her friend and getting her man back to one of the local women who was standing behind her table selling her goods. Immediately, the local woman with the colorful dress and matching turban seemed to know what Jackie had in mind. Without hesitation, she bent under her table, pulled out a packet, and gave it to Jackie. Jackie then handed me the packet with the directions for cleaning your floors or getting your man back.

"Really?" I said. "Is this what I've resorted to?"

A few months later, Bill and I decided to take one last vacation to see if we could work out our marriage or move to divorce. I know going on vacation to work out our divorce has an incongruity to it. We were very confused! To add to our insanity, I brought along the magic potion. As per the instructions, I asked Bill to take a bath in which I'd put half of the power; the other half, I was instructed to use. Then he was to say some words about casting out the other woman or something. We laughed as we did this ritual and didn't think too much about it other than that it was fun and a comic distraction.

When Bill and I returned from vacation, we still weren't getting anywhere, so we gave a therapist from New York City a try. I had spoken to her several times, and so had Bill, independent of my visits. The therapist, a wisp of a woman with long red hair and a dancer's body, was direct. She called it as she saw it. Her belief was that marriage is a spiritual journey. Bill and I walked into her funky, uptown office to devise a plan to finally split for good. Instead, we walked out having agreed to a six-week trial reconciliation.

The Intelligence of the Heart

Finally, our year of heartache was over. Although we hadn't recognized it then, we had received support from the people around us. The professionals, friends, family, and even the ways of magic saw something in us that we had lost sight of: our love for each other. As difficult as it was, time apart from each other was necessary. We needed to grow, and we weren't doing it together. Bill and I had lost our appreciation of each other. When we got back together, we stopped looking for what was wrong with the other person and our marriage and started to validate what was right. We now realized our marriage was an entity in and of itself that needed to be nurtured. If our marriage were treated as nothing, it would become nothing.

We started to clearly state our intentions for our marriage each year with a ritual. We created an "Anniversary Dream Jar." Each year on our anniversary, we put our agreed desire for our marriage into this bottle. On the days before our anniversary, we think about our intention for our marriage. Then when we come together on our anniversary, we discuss and agree on our shared goal, write it on colorful paper, date it, and put it into our bejeweled glass corked bottle. Our intentions may not be immediately realized, but they have always been achieved as long as we are clear.

One of our more challenging desires was to have children. Since I had a fertility problem, I didn't have the confidence to state what I wanted; clearly, I danced around it. To admit how much I wanted children was frightening. What if we couldn't ever have them? To accept it would be to open myself up to experiencing a loss that I didn't want to experience again.

On the other hand, if I didn't say how much I wanted them, I could fool myself into thinking it didn't matter. So one year, we wrote "to create something together." That goal was sufficiently vague that we would be successful for sure, but it didn't produce the child I wanted. Even in our ritual, we could no longer give halfway to our marriage; we needed to give it our all, to be concise, clear, and committed.

Despite ourselves, Bill and I have now been married fifty years. Our marriage has withstood what many marriages haven't been able to endure. Sometimes, I wonder why we held it together when there was seemingly nothing to hold onto. I don't know the reason for Bill, but I think I am finally getting closer to the answer. I attribute it to an experience I had when we were separated. It was one of those brief moments in time when insight comes to you from out of nowhere. I remember walking down the stairs from our living room to the downstairs den in our home in Yardley. Bill was living in the States and was discussing marrying the woman he was involved with. I was sad but finally knew that if it came to him getting married, it would be difficult for me, but I would and could go on and still be happy. As I made my perfunctory way down the steps, something occurred to me, like a light bulb going on. I suddenly realized that I could and would always love Bill, no matter what. That there need not be any conditions to my love. He could even be married to someone else, and I could continue to love him; no one or nothing could take that away from me. I felt my heart open. I was open and peaceful with that thought.

Once again, I was being led by my heart to a place that didn't make much sense to my head or probably anyone else's. This isn't how it's usually done when a couple breaks up. If I'd shared this with my friends or family, at best they'd have thought I was only kidding myself. So I decided to keep this decision to myself, not share it. It is only now that I am bringing it forward, since it's important to see how, once again, for whatever reason, I was allowing myself to trust and be led by the intelligence of my heart. Somehow, some way, my heart knew better than my mind that my path was with Bill. We weren't finished. We had more to do with this life than either of us could see from where we stood. A journey so rich in love, hope, challenges, joy, tears, and an abundance of laughter that we couldn't have dreamed it for ourselves. The best for us was indeed yet to come.

Return to Romania, August 1991

I headed back to Romania, my INS approval giving me a sense of confidence similar to the lion in *The Wizard of Oz*. He got his courage from a badge pinned on him. I got mine from a piece of paper with checkmarks, hopefully in the right places. I had spoken with my lawyer before I left and was assured that although our case didn't fit into the new adoption law, we would be given special consideration.

Bill and I decided we should act fast. I left just a few days later and arrived in Romania on August 14. My entrance into the country felt so different from my first flight here eight months prior. There seemed to be more lights below as we flew over the country. The soldiers on the tarmac still had rifles but looked a little bit more friendly. The weather was warm as opposed to the bone-chilling cold I'd felt last January. I instantly felt more positive—not because I am a warm-weather person, but because I was heading into familiar territory. I knew the airport, the city of Bucharest, a little of the language and ways of the people. I can handle this,

I thought. I can even handle the dreaded taxi driver who for sure wouldn't allow the windows to be opened on this warm August day for fear of the draft, or would try to charge me twice the fare. On my way out of the airport, I checked out the exchange rate, only to decide they were asking too much; I would use the black market to change my money when I got to my hotel.

The first call I made from my hotel was to the US embassy to schedule an appointment with Consul Virginia White. She set up the appointment but told me over the phone that my adoption was never going to happen. Momentarily, the wind was taken out of my sails, but like the lion, I reached for my INS approval and kept our appointment the next day. When I met with Virginia, she recognized my face, saw my five books of documents, and understood the seriousness of my mission.

After she looked it all over, she reluctantly said, "There's a slight chance that this adoption could happen."

I responded most determinedly, "I'll have to go with that."

I walked out of that meeting holding back tears, not letting her know how shaken I was. This was not a time for crying. I knew I was being judged every moment, and I needed to appear strong to be taken seriously.

Later in the day, I was picked up by Laura's parents (Laura was one of the nurses from Casa) and taken to Constanta and Casa Speranta; it was a long, bumpy three-hour ride. Again, I felt more confident because

I knew how much to pay them for the day. In the past, I would have had a long, awkward conversation about how much I wanted to give them as opposed to how much they charged. Romanians considered it impolite to speak of or ask for money, which made for difficult conversations.

When I arrived at Casa Speranta, the American volunteers and the Romanian staff came out of their apartments to greet me. There were lots of hugs, kisses on both cheeks, and fast conversation I didn't understand. But I understood that they were telling me about my children. It was well after nine at night, and all their children were in bed. Everyone knew what was on my mind. So, after this quick hello, I immediately went to see the children. I didn't even pretend that I wasn't going to wake them up.

They were sleepy, but to my relief, they remembered me. We settled in to play as we always did on our carpet in our small 8×10 room. This room held nothing but a chair and a toy box, but that was all we needed. My heart was filled. Being with them again was better than I could have imagined. They all surprised me with how much they had grown in these last months and how they had matured. The older ones had more words, and the younger ones were making new sounds and being understood. Costin was walking, and Dana-Rica was standing and holding on. Each one had grown and gained weight.

I was thrilled to see these changes but a little sad to have missed any part of their lives. As we were playing on the floor, Costin came and sat on my lap as if to say, "This is my rightful spot; I am the baby." Mihaela came to sit on my lap as well; she was the youngest girl, so it was her rightful place also. Ramona stood or tried to stand on her head for my enjoyment. Ionel gave me a book to read. Dana-Rica picked up her own baby doll and gave it the toy bottle. I now knew I wouldn't be able to leave them again; I had to continue. But, just as I needed the children, I needed Bill in my life; he was a part of me. Adoption was the only way to finally get all the people I loved together. Somewhere along the way, we had become a family.

Cristina was nice enough to make my bedroom with the children ready for me. I was filled with such love; each one was so special. Ramona was a natural caretaker, always aware of the safety of the other children. Sometimes, if one of the children got themselves in trouble, I would look to see if Ramona was watching. Ionel established himself as the leader and seemed to be in charge of where and what our group was going to do. Sometimes we would butt heads as to who was going to take the lead. Mihaela, a daredevil with a strong eye for adventure and the forbidden, kept me on my toes. Dana-Rica's tenacious spirit for keeping up with the other children, despite having half the weight, muscle strength, and height, was inspiring. She worked so hard at everything. Last but by no means least, Costin was all about being the baby. He was the youngest by six months and loved to be held. He couldn't get enough of it. He wouldn't have minded if he were attached to my hip all day as long as he was there; he was a loving, happy boy.

As I put the children back in their cribs, I noticed how good they smelled on this warm summer's evening. I had forgotten this about them. I tucked them in and kissed each one good night. Each child had a different blanket to snuggle with that a friend of Bill's mom had made. I sat in the doorway, watching them fall asleep as I quietly sang "Silent Night" to them. I went to bed hearing the soft breathing of my children in the next room. I felt a feeling I had only known with Bill: this is *how* I belong.

For the next two days, I never left the children. We went to the beach. The shoreline of the Black Sea near where we lived used to be a major tourist destination. Now most of the previously grand hotels were closed or very run down. But the children loved the beach and swimming. There also was one place where we could get pizza. I loved seeing them sitting at the restaurant table, as most kids their age were able to do. But this was still new for them. It had only been six months since every meal they had was from a bottle in a crib, so they still had some skills to work on. Mihaela, at two, still did not eat solid food, so licking her pizza was the best she could do for now.

The park was another favorite place we went to. There was one very small incline that the children loved to run down. We also spent many hours out in our own yard. While I was gone, Chuck had built a glider and a jungle gym. The kids loved them when they weren't broken from the neighborhood kids who were too big for the set. As meager as our playset was, we had the only equipment in the neighborhood, so keeping our neighbors' children off just didn't seem right.

When Monday morning came around, I was anxious and excited about meeting with my lawyer and seeing what needed to happen next. I needed to get our adoption going. I wanted to get the children home to the US, where they could get the medication they needed. We had no idea what the virus was doing to their immune systems. Their health was the biggest concern, but they had developmental delays that needed to be attended to also.

Marolen, Casa's new director, and I took off to meet Sorin, my lawyer, at his chosen location, a restaurant bar across from the courthouse.

When I had called him the previous day, he sounded surprised that I was in Romania, even though I had told him I was coming. When he approached us, I knew I was in trouble. He was sweating and nervous, and ordered a drink right away. It was 10 a.m. After pleasantries, which I had no patience for, he got around to dropping the news. Our case would not be given special consideration; we would need to go through the adoption committee. The adoption committee had put a stop to all international adoptions because of the bad publicity that Romania had received for selling its children. Adoptions were not expected to reopen for at least six months.

I was crushed and angry. But mostly confused.

"Why did you tell me over the phone we would be given an exception? What have you done? Have you even been working on my case? What will we do now? Who made this decision?" I quickly shot one question after another at him.

When I slowed down, Marolen picked up the ball. "When was this decision made? When can Susan speak directly with that person? It was the president of the court? Does the president of the court understand the children's health?"

In unison, we said, "We want to speak with the president of the court today!"

Marolen and I left the bar with my very unhappy lawyer and went across the road to see the president of the court (POC). It quickly became very clear that my lawyer had not been to the court on my behalf and had not spoken to the POC. We waited around the busy court as he now tried to get the POC to see us. While we were waiting, we met an Englishman, Miles, who was also waiting to speak with the POC. Marolen and I quickly got him aside to find out if his lawyer was any better than mine. Miles said his lawyer was worse, if that was possible. As we waited for my lawyer and the POC for what felt like an eternity, we spoke with Miles about the coup that had just taken place in Russia and what that might mean for Romania. This was an attempted coup against Gorbachev led by hardline communist members of the Soviet government. Miles also had a translator with him, Chico. Chico offered his opinion about the coup and also slipped into the conversation that he was available to translate my many documents.

Finally, the POC and Sorin returned. After a very confusing conversation translated by Chico, a date was set for court. The POC insisted that we first get the adoption committee's approval. I hired Chico to translate the documents and to go with me to get official permission from the families. It was a productive but extremely frustrating day. I realized I had a long process ahead of me. It was time to get back to the kids to heal my aching spirit.

In the days to come, I had the opportunity to meet with Dr. Matusa. She offered to go with me to my meeting with Dr. Zugravescu, the head of the Romanian adoption committee. She recounted to me in detail the call she made to set up the appointment.

Dr. Zugravescu: *Are you aware that the children must be on a six-month waiting list?*

Dr. Matusa: *Yes.*

Dr. Z: *You know that no adoptions are being heard?*

Dr. M: *Yes.*

Dr. Z: *You know that anyone with HIV is prohibited from entering the US?*

Dr. M: *Yes.*

Dr. Z: *And you know the US does not allow the adoption of any child that has two parents?*

Dr. M: *Yes.*

Dr. Z: *And you still want this meeting?*

Dr. M: *Yes.*

Although what Dr. Matusa reported was not at all encouraging, she didn't seem to be backing off her willingness to take me to Bucharest to attend my meeting with Dr. Z. In the midst of all this discouraging news, I was feeling so supported by this petite warrior woman and committed doctor.

Over the next couple of weeks, two things happened. The first was that Dr. Matusa received written permission for Mihaela to be adopted. This was great news. She was the first, and Dr. Matusa had taken care of it all. The second was my meeting with Dr. Z.

Dr. Matusa and her husband picked me up at Casa Speranta early in the morning. They were driving a Dacia, of course; it was the only car that Romanians had available to buy during the years of Ceaușescu. With my very limited Romanian, our conversation was brief. There wasn't much need for words; the look on Dr. Matusa's face when she saw what I was wearing to the meeting told me plenty. Any girl who has had a mother disapprove of her outfit knows the look. I was wearing a lime green sundress and sandals. I was way too casual for Dr. Matusa. This was the dressiest clothing I had brought with me to Romania. But after the good doctor's look, I made a note to buy or borrow something more business-like if there was a next meeting.

When we got to Bucharest, the doctor's husband dropped us off in front of a gray Soviet-style office building. What I recall about the office space was that it was dark with a large waiting room. There was a desk for her assistant, a young woman with blonde curly hair. She told us to sit while we waited for our appointment.

In Romanian, the expression to sit sounds much more like a demand than an invitation. There was a coldness in the air even though it was warm outside. Her assistant invited us into Dr. Z's office. Dr. Z greeted us and then sat behind her large oak desk. As she walked, I noticed her chunky black shoes, mid-calf black skirt, and pulled-back hair. Her look was very Eastern European. Dr. Matusa and Dr. Z exchanged pleasantries, Romanian style, but Dr. Z barely addressed me. Then they spoke about the children's health, the project at Casa Speranta, and my wish to adopt. I sat quietly to the left of Dr. Matusa, listening carefully to their conversation, trying to piece together Romanian words that I knew.

Finally, Dr. Z turned to me and spoke in Romanian. I already felt like she didn't like me. I wasn't sure why, since I hadn't said anything; it might have been because I was American. As she spoke, Dr. Matusa quickly translated.

She said, "This adoption isn't possible."

I responded, "But who will care for these children?" I was thinking about their lives spent in cribs.

Dr. Z said, just shy of contempt, "This is not your problem. These are Romania's children. We will care for them."

This was the end of the meeting. We were escorted out by her curly-haired assistant, who it seemed did speak English but hadn't used it. I don't know if I made it up, but it felt like her assistant was overly kind on our way out to make up for the curtness of her boss.

Looking back on that time now, I wonder if there was a bit of arrogance about me, an attitude coming from the fact that I came from a country where we believe anything is possible. Did I carry that attitude in my body and communicate that without even speaking? Maybe.

But it's also possible there was something else going on. It comes from being a mother. It is determination. When it comes to caring for and protecting our children, we are blind to interference. We do whatever we need to do to protect our young. Since I had returned to Romania, I had become my children's mother. When Dr. Z told me this adoption was not possible, what I heard was, "I can't or won't do this for you . . . you need to ask someone else."

So before I left Dr. Z's office, I already had that next person in mind.

Dr. Lacatusu was a contact that Brother Toby had given to me. Toby had told me he'd been very helpful in getting Casa Speranta set up. Casa Speranta had been, and to some extent still is, part of the Municipal Hospital in Constanta. I wasn't privy to all that went on to allow an American organization to take over the care of the children that were placed there, but I do know that it was the work of Dr. Matusa and Brother Toby that ultimately made it happen. Dr. Matusa was the head of infectious disease at the hospital, and Brother Toby's care for infected Romanian children in the United States, plus his law degree, made their duo successful. Dr. Lacatusu was one of the officials who championed their cause.

Again, I'm not sure why, but I wasn't intimidated by meeting with these high officials when it came to the children. Dr. Lacatusu was friendly and as supportive as he could be. He suggested that I speak with the other committee members, the Minister of Health and the Minister of Justice, because ultimately it would be their decision since they were members of the adoption committee.

So my journey continued.

Parent Visits

Now faced with the most important part of the adoption, receiving permission from the children's parents, I was terrified. Would the parents say yes? What would it be like? Would they be angry that I asked, or sad or uncaring? As much as I wanted the children, this whole process of asking for someone's child was making me feel sick to my stomach. I had an idea about Mihaela from Dr. Matusa's discussion with her parents. It seemed they had agreed, but with a topic this sensitive, I knew better than to count on it. This experience was surreal and beyond what I thought I was capable of.

When we first arrived at Casa Speranta, the other volunteers and I were very critical when we realized that most of our children weren't orphans. In many cases, they had two parents; and yet rarely, if ever, did a parent come to visit. I judged these parents harshly until one day when I was trying to put down a crying child who did not want to let go. I had a realization that if this had been my child, I didn't know if I would have been able to come to visit, knowing that I would only leave them again. Such pain for me but even more so for the child who, at two years old, has no understanding, only a strong need to be touched, held, and loved. How traumatic would that experience be for the child? Would separating again and again traumatize them even more?

So when it came to the parents of my children, I tried not to judge. I did the best I could trying to remember "until you walk a mile in someone's shoes . . . ," but when a set of parents expressed no concern for their child, I judged. One family never asked about their child, whom they hadn't seen in over a year, but instead showed me, with so much love and pride, their cow. I judged them. And finally, another family asked for money in exchange for their child; I was angry, and I judged.

Ramona

My first experience of asking a couple to adopt their child had me in a state of fear and anxiety. Ramona's family was from a town not far from Constanta. The day I went to meet them, Dr. Matusa picked me up. She needed Ramona's family to sign papers allowing the American volunteers to care for her. She thought it was a good time to broach the subject of adoption.

The family lived and worked on a large farm owned by the state. They lived in a barn close to the front of the farm. They had no electricity or running water, from what I could tell, although we were never invited inside. I caught a glance of their living space as we spoke. I learned that they had nine other children, and Ramona was number ten. Both parents were about my age, and they had been together for many years but never married. They seemed only to have the clothes on their backs. The mom was small, probably just under five feet tall. She had dark skin, whether from the sun or her ethnicity, I wasn't sure. There were many gypsies in Romania and many at Casa Speranta, but Ramona was never referred to as such. The Romanians have a strong prejudice against gypsies. Ramona's mother wore a babushka, a plain skirt, and many sweaters; her hands spoke of hard work and hard life. Although she wasn't very tall, she was stocky and looked strong. The father was a "big hat, no cattle" kind of guy. He was about the same size as her and wore a cap cocked to the side. As he took charge of the conversation, he seemed to want to impress us as he puffed out his chest. His demeanor felt as out of place as a puffer fish on a farm. In the months to come, I would come to understand why he needed to show off his place of authority and why his body was so frail: he had a bad drinking problem. This problem was so bad that he was so inebriated one evening when I visited to get some papers signed that he needed to be held up to make his mark. And since there was no electricity where they lived, this was done by the headlights of the car.

The day we first visited, Dr. Matusa spoke on my behalf. I could follow much of the conversation, but there didn't seem to be much emotion from either of them. I caught a glimpse of a couple of kids staring at us as we stood outside the barn and spoke. One of them, about twelve, looked just like I imagined Ramona would look at that age. Cute. After what seemed like a short, agreeable conversation, the father signed Dr. Matusa's papers, and he led us to a large concrete area. He explained that this area had recently been filled with cattle that had died during the winter from starvation. This was where he burned the carcasses. At this point, the mood turned very solemn, and I started to realize I had no idea what life was like for these people. I could not imagine Ramona, who at four years of age had a "valley girl" vibe, living under these harsh conditions. I said an awkward goodbye to the mother. I wasn't feeling a strong connection with her, although I wanted to. The father walked us to our car in his robust manner; he gave Dr. Matusa and me a kiss on the hand, a Romanian-style kiss for goodbye.

On the trip back to Casa Speranta, I learned from Dr. Matusa that the couple was considering the adoption, but Dr. Matusa had a feeling that they might allow it. She had spoken to them about it being an opportunity for Ramona to get medication for HIV that wasn't available in Romania, and that this adoption might save her life. I started to feel encouraged and terrified at the same time. I learned that Ramona had never left the hospital since the day she was born, and she had been very small and sick at birth. Her parents didn't offer any other information about her. Romania had outlawed contraception during the reign of Ceaușescu, and this family was just another one that had been made to have children they could not care for. The journalist Wendell Steavenson described the Romanian government's coercive measures to increase the country's birth rate in a 2014 article in the *Guardian*:

> *Motherhood became a state duty. The system was ruthlessly enforced by the secret police, the securitate. Doctors who performed abortions were imprisoned, women were examined every three months in their workplaces for signs of pregnancy. If they were found to be pregnant and didn't subsequently give birth, they could face prosecution. Fertility had become an instrument of state control.*[*]

Ceaușescu took this stand against any form of contraception because he wanted to build the workforce. By building their population, he felt he would have enough workers to prevent the country from carrying any national debt:

> *Romanian leader Nicolae Ceaușescu announced this week that his country, despite an economy that a recent U.S. congressional report called the second poorest in Europe, has paid off all of its foreign debts ahead of schedule. The costs of this accelerated repayment program have been massive. In a recent report on Romanian human rights violations, congressional Helsinki Commission chairman Rep. Steny H. Hoyer (D-Md.) and Sen. Dennis DeConcini (D-Ariz.) wrote: "Fuel and electricity have been rationed for years. Staple foods,*

---

[*] Wendell Steavenson, "Ceaușescu's Children," *The Guardian*, December 10, 2014, *https://www.theguardian.com/news/2014/dec/10/-sp-ceausescus-children*.

> *including milk, bread and flour, are rationed, and
> in many localities even these are unavailable. Meat
> is a rarity; soup bones only occasionally appear in
> stores. Decades of financial misplanning and inef-
> ficient industrial development have led to the dire
> condition of the Romanian economy, making it the
> poorest in Europe after Albania."*[**]

Ramona's family was so poor and had so many children they could barely survive. So it wasn't too big of
a surprise when further into this process, the father
asked for money in exchange for his daughter.

Dana-Rica/Loredana

I hadn't been looking forward to Dana-Rica's family
visit. I found that the visit to Ramona's family was
upsetting for days before and after the actual visit. It
was so difficult not knowing what kind of response I
might get. There was no way to predict how a family
would react to an American woman coming to their
door and asking to adopt their child. It was a situation
that no one could ever imagine for themselves. Sometimes, when I thought of what I was actually doing, I
thought about how arrogant I must be. Did I think
I could do better for their child than they could? *But
they aren't with their families,* I thought. Today, I was

[**] A. D. Horne, "Debts Paid, Romania Says," *Washington Post,* April
14, 1989, *https://www.washingtonpost.com/archive/politics/1989
/04/14/debts-paid-romania-says/89557c5f-9f4d-4810-8e15
-91538f134a3f/.*

filled with dread at a possible negative response from Dana-Rica's family. Adding to my apprehension, Dr. Matusa was unavailable to go with me. Chico was with me instead. He was very good at translating, but I felt that Dr. Matusa would have given me more credibility.

For the excursion, I arranged for Danny, the same driver that had met Bill at the airport months ago, to take us to Dana-Rica's family. Danny, like everyone else, drove a Dacia. Most of the cars on the road now showed Romania's years of poverty. In our short drive, we came across several Dacias sitting by the roadside, waiting for their owners to repair them and get them going for a few more trips. So I was happy to see that when I got into our Dacia, it was in good shape and worthy of the drive.

It wasn't a bad drive from Constanta to Dana-Rica's parents' house. They lived outside of Cernavoda, another Soviet-style city with numerous grayish apartment blocks. It was also the home of a new nuclear power plant that formed the skyline of the city and could be seen from the family's house. From the little village where Dana-Rica's parents lived, it was one long road to Cernavoda and the towers of the nuclear plant. If I let my imagination run wild, I could see it as the Yellow Brick Road leading to Emerald City. Their small gray stucco house was set back off the road and had a garden and a cow, both of which were used to sustain the couple. In the official paperwork, the home was referred to as "abnormal living conditions." It was meager, but it was well cared for.

We were lucky to find the couple at home since they didn't have a phone to set up an appointment Chico took the initiative to introduce us and let them know that we were there to speak about their daughter. The couple were very small people, like their daughter, which led me to believe we had found the right parents. They both seemed to be in their late thirties or early forties, were just under five feet tall, and looked amazingly alike, with prominent noses, similarly shaped eyes, and brownish hair. Their skin was darkish, probably from work outside. They could have passed for brother and sister.

It was difficult speaking about something so sensitive as the adoption of their child, especially when I was depending on someone else to communicate for me. But Chico seemed to establish a rapport easily with the couple, which I was very grateful for. They told us that at the present time, they were both unemployed. I am unsure why he wasn't employed, but she was pregnant. She spoke with pride about her work at the power plant. Pride in this plant was an attitude shared by many. It was being built by Romanians and Canadians together. It had been a long time since this country, which had been left so far behind, had something to feel proud of. Our conversation with the father seemed to revolve around his complaints about the state of economic conditions in Romania and his pride in his cow. We finally got around to speaking about Dana-Rica and my intention to adopt her. It was not lost on me that this was the first the couple had spoken of their daughter, even though we had clearly spoken of our intention when we arrived.

"She had been lost at the hospital," they said. I knew she was very small, but could this be true? How do you lose a child at the hospital? These were my thoughts as I listened to Chico speak to Dana-Rica's parents.

For sure, this child was a confusing child—even her name and her age were unclear. Born weighing eight hundred grams, just less than two pounds, Loredana— the name we learned she was given at birth—was too small to leave the hospital. Her parents said, "This was the last we saw her. When we went back to the hospital, she wasn't there." I was so confused. How did her name change, and how is a child lost at the hospital? I had been told that her name was Dana-Rica Vasili. However, now her birth papers stated that her last name was Dinu (the father's name), and her first name was Loredana, not Dana-Rica. They didn't know why the first name was so different, but the confusion over the last name came from the fact that Loredana's parents never married. The hospital must have thought that she carried the last name of the mother, but apparently, she had been given her father's name. I guess losing her at the hospital was plausible because of overcrowding; children were easily transferred to another hospital. It took a while to get this information sorted out. Once we finally understood, the conversation went easily, and we left their home with their approval of the adoption. I was ecstatic! This was really going to happen. Dana-Rica, who from now on we called by her birth name, Loredana, was going to be mine. I was so thankful. I was grateful for having someone like Chico who was sympathetic to my intentions.

I told the couple that I intended to return with additional papers to be signed in a few weeks. This second visit took longer than I expected to arrange because of the holdup with the Romanian adoption committee. When I returned, I brought clothes for the new baby and was excited to see this new child, but that baby didn't return from the hospital either. Although the couple didn't offer any additional information about the baby, my translator and I left with the feeling that this was another child that had been left to the state to care for.

As we were leaving and saying our goodbyes, I noticed that the father had pulled Chico aside to tell him something. When we got back into the car, he told me that the father had asked that we buy him a cassette player to help him remember his child. I was immediately filled with anger. How dare he! She could not be so easily replaced. It was clear that he had taken some advice from someone. I guess I should have been impressed that he was asking for so little. *But then again, she's a very small child,* I thought, smiling. I knew that this exchange wasn't going to take place; children were not to be paid for. Thankfully this request did not come up again or interfere with our adoption.

There was nothing easy about the severe poverty created by the dictator Ceaușescu and the decisions it led this couple to make. There were many times during this long, drawn-out process that I tried to remember, once again, that until I had walked in their shoes, I would never know what their life was like.

Costin

Dr. Matusa was championing our cause to get Ramona and Mihaela's parents to give us their permission. She had just received an affirmative response from Mihaela's family. She had also been in touch with Ionel's family, but I wasn't as sure where they were with the adoption. They lived eight to ten hours north of Constanta without a phone, so communicating with them was difficult. We were waiting to hear from them after Dr. Matusa had written them about our intentions.

Now it was time to speak with Costin's family. It was just the two of us for this trip. Dr. Matusa said her husband needed to work. They are a really cute couple, and he is a good driver, but it was nice to have the car trip alone with her. Costin lived about forty minutes away in Medgidia. I was feeling calm and positive about this visit. Loredana's visit wasn't so bad. I felt like I could handle it.

As we entered the town of Medgidia, we passed many small, gray houses made of concrete. The homes had short brick walls around them. Many of them had small gardens and grape barbs in the yards. They were very sweet. They looked very old-world, built before Soviet-era apartment buildings. This was in contrast to Constanta, which had mostly gray, austere, Soviet bloc apartments that Caucșescu had ordered built. These apartments were his attempt to modernize the city. But taking down small homes like these had stripped the city of its warmth and character. As we drove on, we passed horses pulling wooden wagons with goods on them and country women dressed mostly in black with scarves tied under their chins. We also maneuvered around loose chickens, street dogs, and kids. I had my first experience of seeing a pig being prepared in the street. I never got the chance to watch the whole process, but I know that the family first burned the hair off the pig. Then they cut it up to store for later or share with another family that may have contributed to the purchase. This whole process was a big deal, and the meat would last quite a while. At Christmas and other holidays, anyone who could afford it would buy a pig.

As we drove through the city and got closer to where Dr. Matusa thought Costin's family lived, we stopped a man on the street to ask for directions. We did this by simply asking for the family by name; I never heard an address given. This process of stopping and asking continued about three more times until we reached their home. Since they didn't have a phone and we couldn't call ahead, they were not expecting us.

Their home was much like the other homes we had passed. There were steps leading to their upstairs room; I think the grandparents lived downstairs. Neighborhood boys, about five to ten years old, played in the street out front. They didn't seem to have any particular game going aside from tormenting each other. It was a Saturday, so they were dressed in their raggediest and acting accordingly.

As we drove up, all the kids' attention focused on us. They led us to the house while shooting questions at me about America. Dr. Matusa gave them a look that must have said stop; then they were off like a shot.

I wondered, *How do they always know I'm American?*

Costin's mother came to the door. She was a very young, shy woman in her early twenties. She knew Dr. Matusa and treated her with deference. She had met Dr. Matusa when she first learned of Costin's illness. Her home was very modest but clean and well cared for. We were told that her husband was down the street at the bar, but she would send one of the children to get him. As we waited, Dr. Matusa told her about Costin and the care that he was receiving from the American volunteers, as she referred to me. The mom looked me over and made strong eye contact with me, as if by looking at me as if she could read my soul.

Finally, after what seemed like a very long time, the father came running up the stairs. He apologized for keeping us waiting. When he was seated, Dr. Matusa proceeded to express my desire to adopt and gave her opinion as to why she supported it. As she spoke, the couple started to cry, as did I. I started to realize that if I allowed myself to really feel the pain and the grief that this couple was feeling, my own tears would be uncontrollable. All of a sudden, I saw myself as separate from the event, like I was watching it on TV. I no longer felt like I was part of what was going on in the room. I heard Dr. Matusa tell me that the dad had said, "No! I won't let him go. If he is going to die from this disease . . . let him come home here to die."

Was I really part of this? I had never, in my wildest imagination, thought that I might be sitting in someone's house asking to have their child for myself. It was surreal. Who was I to even ask this question? Did I really think I could do better for their child than they could?

The mom kept looking at me, trying to draw something out of me; I wasn't sure what. After many more tears and Romanian conversation that I did not understand, we were finally ready to go. It was decided that the couple would think about my request. There was no good or cheery way to leave. Our sole intention for this meeting was to ask for permission to adopt their child. I left there feeling so drained from the pain of it all. It was pain so raw and thick that even Dr. Matusa, who knew so well about the loss of children, having lost so many to AIDS, was feeling their sadness deeply. We drove for many miles, quietly wiping our tears until we both started to feel calmer. At this point, all I wanted was just to get back to Casa Speranta and to the children. I knew that being with them was what I needed to heal my heart.

As it turned out, only a month later, Costin's family ended up giving permission for us to adopt Costin. Just like the other parents, they came to court to verbally give their permission for the adoption. It was quite the scene in the courtroom, with ten parents and me. I am sure many people in the court wondered, *What is this crazy American thinking? Five children?!* But all the parents gave their permission. Now there were just a few more steps, or so Bill and I thought.

The following week we got the news that would throw us off our path. After one year of feeling and acting like Costin's mom, and having gained his parents' approval, Costin was no longer mine. He was no longer part of our family.

About two months after getting permission from Costin's parents, all the children had to get an updated test for HIV. Costin's test came back negative. He didn't have the virus! It was unbelievable! He must have initially been tested wrong. This was great news. He was going to be okay; we would have a child that was free of this deadly virus. But I wasn't celebrating because I knew what I had to do. I had to call and tell the parents. Even though his parents had given him up through the court, I knew that now that he didn't have the virus, they would be able to care for him and want him back.

The advice of the Romanian women at Casa Speranta was to not tell the parents; the dad drank too much. That was not something I could do. I called his family, and his mom came to get him right away. I had hoped that the mom might stay the night to allow Costin some time to transition, but she wanted him out of there ASAP. I couldn't blame her. Now we were no longer five; Costin was no longer my baby. The kids no longer had a baby brother. I no longer counted to five each time I did something for the children.

This all may sound silly, but I hadn't noticed until he left how many times a day it was 1, 2, 3, 4, 5 spoons; 1, 2, 3, 4, 5 plates; 1, 2, 3, 4, 5 treats, diapers, baths. . . . He had been there, part of us; now he was gone. It happened so quickly. I hurt and had a hole inside of me, but I also knew in my heart that, drinking dad or not, I had done the right thing. Costin belonged with his birth family. I knew what it was like to be separated from your family, and I couldn't have lived with myself had I not told them.

Children of Casa

I was so thankful that my children were healthy, but that was not true for all the children at Casa Speranta. A few of the children came to Casa in the later stages of AIDS. Brother Toby had decided to take symptomatic children at the beginning of the project, when he insisted on taking Loredana against the advice of the doctors. He was unwilling to turn a child away because their life might be short.

As I dealt with all the legal obstacles, I watched what AIDS could do to a child. Since we'd started the previous January at Casa Speranta, we had lost six of the children to this awful disease. I now felt that I knew HIV/AIDS. I saw how it took their energy and their appetite for life and left them with nothing to live on. Seeing what the disease could do made it urgent to get the children's adoption approved and get them to the US. Since my stay in the country, Romania had gone from a country in denial about HIV to realizing how big a problem it was, but it still had no medication to treat patients. In the US, the children would be seen by the foremost leader in the field of pediatric HIV/AIDS. They would have medication available to them that they didn't have in Romania. The legal process I was going through had to move more quickly—the children's lives were at stake.

When Dragos came to live at Casa, he already had a look about him that made you feel that he was not of this world. His curly blonde hair, blue eyes, and tall, thin body gave the three-year-old an angelic look. You had to look twice to be sure he was real. Dragos was so good and kind. He would lie on a mattress on the floor as the other children played around him, never raising his voice or complaining. One day, only months after he arrived, he left this world and his life as quietly as he had lived it.

If Dragos was like salt, Aska was like pepper. A two-year-old with dark brown hair, eyes, and skin, she was spicy and vibrant. If you saw Dragos for only a few minutes, you might have forgotten he was there. But with only a little bit of Aska, like it or not, you knew she was there. Everyone had an opinion of her. Some of the staff thought that she was wild. Early on, she learned to climb out of her crib and find very creative ways to entertain herself. Aska might get in another child's crib to play in the middle of the night or paint the room with a blue antiseptic. Ideas like these came easily to her and spiced up life at Casa.

Many a day, when Aska was still on the main ward and not yet placed in a family, I came down to the kitchen in the morning and found her standing on her head, as best she could, in her crib, looking at the world upside down. She actually spent an amazing amount of time like that. I thought she might be saying to herself, *This situation is too messed up. This is not how kids should live; let me look at it another way. Maybe if I'm upside down, it will look better.*

Like many of the children with AIDS, Aska started to waste away. It was called "failure to thrive." As she lost her battle against AIDS, she also lost her spice; it hurt in the pit of my stomach to see. Aska was the second child to leave us.

Guilsey was a very petite, dark-haired, brown-eyed, three-year-old girl. She was said to be a gypsy. In Romania, gypsies were looked down on and said to be dirty and thieves, among other things. When it came to caring for children with AIDS, this prejudice had no home at Casa. We had many gypsy children.

If she had been old enough, Guilsey would have been the leader of our group of children. She was Marolen's child. When she came to Casa, she immediately took over Marolen and Marolen's heart. Since Marolen was the director of Casa Speranta, her work sometimes took her away from home, but Guilsey was attached to her hip when she was there. This little bit of a girl was strong-willed. She knew what she wanted; and if she wanted something, she usually wanted it now. There were many times when there would be a war of wills between her and Marolen. I believe that it was her will that kept her small body going as long as it did.

But the virus came for Guilsey, and as much as she fought it, when she was four it took charge. She started to lose weight and her desire to interact with the other children. The only thing she didn't lose was her fight; if she didn't want something, like food or a toy, it might come flying back at you. One day toward the end of her life, one of the children saw her lying down instead of playing.

They said to their friend, "Guilsey is going to live with God."

Guilsey immediately sat up and said, "No! I'm not going."

This statement got me wondering if I was misleading my children when I told them you only die when you are ready. I had not been with Guilsey when she died, so I asked Marolen.

"Was Guilsey ready? Was she at peace when she died?" I asked.

Marolen said, "Yes, she was, but it took her a long time to get there. She fought almost to the end."

Marlon's words reminded me of a quote, "We die the way we lived." Which makes sense; why would we die any differently than we lived? Guilsey was a fighter; she fought for her life as long as possible.

Then there was Valie, a little one-and-a-half-year-old girl who was part of Marolen's family. She was a round, plump little girl who was quiet and shy. Each night to put herself to sleep, she would rock and knock her head against the crib. She did this with such force that the pounding could be heard down the hall. The impact caused her to have a constant hematoma on her forehead.

In our attempt to help her, we decided to move her bed to the floor. We believed that this for sure would protect her from hurting herself anymore. It was difficult to get her to settle down, but after we rubbed her back and sang to her, she fell asleep. But in her distorted way of trying to soothe herself, in the night she crawled over to the crib and went back to knocking her head on the outside of it. This was what she knew; this was comfort.

I often think of Valie when my life is feeling hard. Am I stuck in an old pattern? A pattern that is hurting me? Do I continue to hurt myself just because it is familiar to me?

At this point in the process, I couldn't have felt more stuck. I was constantly in pain . . . pain that I had brought on myself.

The parents had all given their permission. They had all been to court. But nothing more could happen until the adoption committee gave their consent. It seemed to be a waiting game. One of the women that worked at Casa tried to encourage me by telling me I was learning patience. This is a quality that I must say I never saw the value in. Like Valie, my head constantly hurt. Was I knocking my head against the wall?

Thanksgiving 1991

During the third week of November 1991, I returned home to Princeton for a quick visit and to celebrate Thanksgiving with Bill. Simona and Cristina had agreed to watch the children while I was gone. Bill and I needed the time together. I had left my home in Princeton in August with misinformation from my lawyer that our adoption was much further along than it was. I had believed that my trip to Romania would be short. I would go to court, present my documents, and return to the US with the children. But that was not how it was going.

I had been there for three months, and the end was nowhere in sight. Emotionally, Bill and I had not been prepared for another long separation. I was depressed and frustrated by the Romanian system that was being redesigned in the process of our adoption. To make matters worse, Dr. Zugravescu, the head of the Romanian adoption committee, took an immediate dislike to me, which made getting appointments with her difficult. I often felt that she sent me out like Dorothy in search of the broomstick when she would tell me to get a signature, a stamp on a document, or approval of some official after meeting her requirements from the previous time. Her negative attitude toward me was voiced by her assistant when I called to ask for an introduction to the health minister. Dr. Zugravescu had requested that I get his approval for the adoption.

Her assistant said, "Dr. Zugravescu is not willing to help you in any way. She does not trust your intentions with the children."

This statement was hard to hear since it was a personal attack, and it made me doubt that the adoption would ever be approved with Dr. Zugravescu as the head of the adoption committee. It was now November, and it had been three and a half months since I returned to Romania. This situation was leaving me feeling heavy and trapped. I would often think, as I looked at the gray sky, that these low thick clouds hanging over Romania seemed too difficult to get through. I could break myself out, as I was doing for Thanksgiving, but I couldn't see the way to getting us all out. The clouds felt oppressive, holding us down. I needed the heaviness to lift, the clouds to open to the blue sky so that we could all fly out.

My visit home was a mixed bag of feelings with many highs and lows. Seeing Bill was a high point. He and I were filled with such passion when we met at the airport. My love for him felt so deep. So many times I'd had to push away feelings of longing for him, knowing I couldn't let them in or I would never be able to complete the adoption. Now, I basked in knowing that when I needed to have him close to me, he was right there. Over the next four days, my time with him went so quickly; like teenagers, our need for physical touch never stopped.

But entering our home was altogether another feeling. Instead of the warmth and welcome I might have expected, our home felt different, cold, untouched, like a museum. The pieces were all where they belonged, but there was no energy or life in them. There was loneliness to our family home. I didn't need to ask Bill how it had been for him: I could feel it. A little of the warmth that I was missing came pounding around the corner as Falkor, our golden retriever, came to check out who was there. When I saw him, the tears that I had been holding back came rushing forward. He represented all that I had been missing: Bill, my home, my family, my friends, my dog. As he danced around me with abandon, I sobbed deep inside. It felt as though this release was from the last year of so much unexpressed sadness being separated from those I loved.

Over the few days that I was home, I visited friends and caught up with those I couldn't connect with over the phone. Everyone wanted to know about the adoption. And much to our surprise, suddenly our friends were offering their opinions; it was becoming very real to them. Very quickly, Bill and I learned not to open a discussion with friends we felt were not supportive of our decision. We needed to stay as positive as we could.

For Thanksgiving, we were invited along with Bill's parents to my older brother Charlie's house. We took our more spacious car for the hour's drive to Chatham,

New Jersey. We had packed all the pies we had made and a mince that we had cheated and bought. Bill's gray-haired eighty-year-old father and seventy-six-year-old mother were in the back seat; Bill was driving.

Although I wasn't going to have all the work for Thanksgiving, I was going to miss some of the rituals. Every Thanksgiving, my father-in-law and I would get up early to stuff the turkey and get it in the oven. Every year we approached the task as if it had never been done before.

Bill's dad would say, "I don't think we should cover that bird, Sue."

I would respond, "No, Dad, I think we do. We take it off toward the end."

From there, our conversation would go to all our mistakes and triumphs with the birds of past years. Like the time we had to throw the whole turkey out and get sandwiches because Bill's sister got caught in a snowstorm and showed up twelve hours late. We left the stuffed turkey out, forgetting it had been stuffed with sausage.

Bill's father would also share many stories from when he was young as we drank our coffee, peeled potatoes, and such. He would also tell me his favorite funny story about the man who went to fix his roof. The man tied a rope around the bumper of his car, threw it around his chimney, and tied it around himself in case of a fall. His wife came out to go to the store and unknowingly backed the car out of the driveway.

Although I heard this same story every year, I loved hearing it again. It was part of our ritual.

But this Thanksgiving, it became clear that Bill's parents were not in favor of the adoption. Their reasons were twofold. First and foremost, they feared the pain we would endure with the possible loss of so many children. And financially, how could we take on the medical expenses that the children might incur? Over the few days that they had been staying with us, they had tiptoed around their displeasure. Many times the conversation was directed at me since they felt I was the deciding factor.

One morning when it was just us two, Bill's mom asked me, "Won't the expense of the children put additional pressure on Bill financially?"

I chose not to respond to this question because I knew it was more her expressing her concern than wanting an answer from me. Since today was a holiday, I thought we were off the hook for the day.

But as we were pulling out of the driveway, Bill's father said, "You know, Susan, I pray every day that this adoption doesn't go through."

I saw red. To the man I loved and considered my father, who I had never raised my voice to, I responded in anger, "How dare you! This is God's decision, not yours."

There was quiet in the car for the next fifty-eight minutes of the trip. My response may not seem so harsh, but to my father-in-law, it was. He treated me as one of his own, and I could do no wrong. To go against his will was something I had never done. Also, he was a religious man; to bring to question God's will over his might have been going too far. It hurt me deeply to have spoken to him in that tone. I surprised myself with this exchange as I realized how much I had become the children's mother. I was fighting for them with every inch of my being.

The day after Thanksgiving, I got a very upsetting call from Kate, one of my very best friends. Choking back her tears, I heard her say, "Susan, Christopher has died in a car accident." Christopher was her twenty-one-year-old son.

I didn't need to hear any more. I told her, "I'll be right there." And I was out the door.

Before I left to volunteer in Romania, Kate and I had walked the towpath at the canal every day for the last five years. We knew just about everything about each other. We experienced all ways of being together—serious, silly, angry, hopeful, patient, impatient—and we laughed and cried at a moment's notice. Now I was going to her when I knew that she was feeling grief so deep, and I couldn't go there: I didn't have the means to go there. The only vehicle that could bring someone there was to have had the same experience themselves, the loss of a child. With that knowledge, I did the best I could to be with her and receive her pain. But I was leaving in a day and a half. I only had a limited amount of coverage for the care of the children. I would not be able to support Kate through this devastating time. I would not be able to attend the services for her son or be there day and night when she might need to talk or cry. Taking care of her would go to her other friends. I hated this; I wanted to be there for her.

Once again, I was learning what it meant to be a mother. The sacrifices that needed to be made. Leaving my friend in her time of need was a big one. Also, I saw through Kate the pain of a mother who had lost a part of herself, her child.

Was life showing me what was in store for me?

Christmas 1991

B y the time I got resettled in Romania, Christmas was almost upon us. And, though it had been a couple of weeks, I still couldn't get used to Costin not being with us. Each day when I'd go into the children's room, it felt so empty. It felt like I was missing a part of my body, like a finger. I could still do what I needed to, but just not as easily or without some pain. And sometimes I'd forget and go to reach for him, and like a missing finger that causes phantom pain, I would feel the pain of him not being there.

The kids and I decorated the apartment for Christmas as best we could with our limited supplies. We pasted paper Santas and stars that the bobbies made on the windows. At the market, we got the skinniest twig of a Christmas tree that I had ever seen. It was one of the nicest ones they had. I was sure Bill would have a lot to say about it, but we loved it. It was our Charlie Brown Christmas tree.

The children were so excited that Tata (the Romanian name for father) was coming. They acted as though they remembered who he was even though they hadn't seen him since Easter. In the cold, we piled out onto the sidewalk to greet him. I knew that this kind of greeting would touch him deeply, and it did. Through the gray of the winter's day, my four little munchkins, dressed in colorful coats, brought life to our home. When Bill arrived, he just stood in awe as the children ran to hug him while shouting, "Tata! Tata!" He hugged them all separately and then together in a group hug as I stood by with tears in my eyes. It looked like from now on, I was going to have to learn to wait my turn to get my hugs.

It was our first Christmas with the children, and Bill and I were so excited we hardly slept the two days before. Christmas Eve, we had a celebration with all the children in the building. It took place in our common area where all our celebrations were held. We had a larger version of our Christmas tree twig in this room. All thirty of the children, dressed in their best, sat around their low tables constructed of expired cough medicine boxes. These boxes were now considered furniture by all. We sang Christmas carols. "Rudolph the Red-Nosed Reindeer" was the favorite by far. Then we heard a "Ho, ho, ho," and it was a visit from Santa. Bill looked very Santa-like in his red suit and beard. All thirty of the children, plus a couple of the Romanian moms, took turns sitting on his lap. When Ramona saw Santa, she immediately shouted out, "Tata, Tata!" When the party was over, Bill told me that being Santa was one of the best experiences of his life. After that, it was story time about Santa and his reindeer, hanging stockings, and leaving milk and cookies out, then bedtime.

I would like to say that the children were excited, but they had no experience of Christmas and what awaited them the next morning. Of course, Bill and I could hardly wait for the first Christmas with our new family. It took all we had to wait for the kids to wake up on Christmas morning. Bill kept an eye on me; he knew that I would be tempted to wake the children by shaking or kicking their cribs.

The children all looked so cute in their new footed sleepers as they sat on the floor to open their gifts. They were a little confused about opening presents but caught on to unwrapping quickly. The children of Casa had a storeroom full of stuffed animals from donations, but they didn't have many toys. Ionel learned easily how to build with his large LEGO blocks. Every time he made a new structure, he came running screaming, "Mommy look, Mommy look!"

Loredana took to her new doll like any mother with her new baby. The doll was just the right size for her. She was dressed in blue PJs with a hood with rabbit ears and fit in Loredana's arms just right. She went everywhere with Loredana; even when Loredana played with her much-coveted stacking cups, the doll had a front-row seat on her lap.

Ramona and Mihaela received dolls, also. It was amazing to see how well they held them, talked to them, and fed them. Since this care was not their experience in life, I wondered how they knew.

Bill and I sat on the floor with our backs against the wall in the wonder of our new family. We still only had one chair in the apartment, which at that moment was being used for sleeping baby dolls. As we gazed at the children, I saw Bill's look of pure joy as he watched Ionel. His boy! Bill had shared with me how the day before, when he and Ionel had walked home from the store, Ionel held his hand the whole way, calling him "Tata" every chance he could. I could tell Bill felt as I did: these kids were ours; there was no going back. With our skimpy tree and few presents, this Christmas was the best Christmas Bill and I had ever experienced.

A Long, Cold Winter

Romania's weather is very similar to the weather I was used to in New Jersey, but although it was familiar, I didn't like it. The darkness and the cold of the winter challenged my mental well-being.

That winter did its best to deliver cold, dark, windy, and depressing. Constanta, which is on the seaport and usually gets little snow, received a major blast. Since I never saw a snow plow, this led to weeks of piled-up black snow that we needed to climb over and slush through. It made the city look how I imagined an old coal mining town covered in soot would look.

Adding to my need for mental fortitude was not knowing if the adoption would ever go through. For the next three months, December through March, I was once again in limbo. It wasn't that I wasn't working on the adoption; I wasn't getting any answers. The Romanian adoption committee had stated that they would reopen by September. Yet, almost half a year later, they had not reopened nor given us a date when they would. I had been to court three times and gotten approval from the families. But the court was also waiting for the adoption committee's decision.

I had been to the clerk's office in each district a child came from in pursuit of stamps for the adoption papers. Everything needed a stamp. The clerk's office was also where I went to get copies of the documents. Under Ceaușescu, the general public couldn't own typewriters and copy machines. The few that were allowed needed to be registered. My interpreter quickly taught me if I wanted something done promptly, it was best to show up with a gift of cigarettes or chocolate.

My longest trip was to Iasi, eight hours away, where Ionel's family lived. We drove for hours only to get to the last quarter mile, where we needed to leave the car by the side of the road and walk through the mud to get to Ionel's family. The road to their home was so deep with mud from the spring thaw that it was difficult to walk. My driver and I were both laughing and cursing when we arrived; we had both lost a shoe in the mud.

Since his family didn't have a phone, they didn't know we were coming. Ionel's mom was stunned to see us. She seemed embarrassed as she stood before the door, not inviting us in. It was not the first time that I had met Ionel's mom. She had come to visit Ionel right before Christmas. I liked her the moment I met her. It saddened me that this young woman didn't have the means, support, or know-how to keep Ionel with her. She clearly loved him and was giving him up out of that love.

We were there to get a document signed, stamped, and copied. So I came well prepared with Romanian cigarettes. We all drove to the clerk's office together; we got the stamps that we needed, and then drove her back and said our goodbyes. Then the driver and I retraced our muddy prints back to the car and headed home. The trip took a little over twenty hours. Although we accomplished what we needed to, it felt very business-like and strange with Ionel's mom; since I didn't have the language I needed, I had to leave it that way.

Aside from spending time with the children and on the adoption process, I wanted to learn about Romania. With this in mind, Marolen and I hired a Romanian language tutor. On winter nights we sat in Marolen's room wrapped in blankets and practiced our Romanian while having a beer and smoking cigarettes. And when we weren't conjugating verbs with our tutor, we were pumping him for information about life before the revolution. Our tutor told us about how hard life was during the time of Ceaușescu, just two short years before. These words from writer Ian Colford explain a little of it:

> Imagine living in a country where the government operates under a shroud of secrecy, where questioning official policy is a punishable offense, where your next-door neighbor or best friend or cousin or brother might be watching and reporting on your activities, where a harmless act or innocuous remark could land you in prison. That's what life was like for people in Eastern Europe for much of the previous century. The fear was real, the threats genuine.[*]

---

[*] Ian Colford, "The Typewriter as Weapon," February 22, 2015, http://www.iancolford.com/blog/2015/6/1/the-typewriter-as-weapon.

Our tutor also gave us other glimpses into this not-so-distant past.

One day, he asked us, "Do you know that Ceaușescu only had four years of school?" I could tell from his demeanor he was really telling us, not asking.

He went on by saying, "State television, which broadcast just two hours a day, reported mainly on the 'hero of the nation,' Ceaușescu. You were only allowed one sixty-watt light per room; bridge clubs and other clubs were not allowed to meet (too many intellectuals together); everything was rationed—bread, meat, and gasoline. Sometimes people would need to wait up to forty-eight hours to get gas."

He took a breath and continued. "Ceaușescu rationed everything in an attempt to lower the national debt." He then spoke about the restrictions on contraception and abortion, the consequences of which we were fully aware: families were forced by law to have children they could not care for in order to build the workforce. These regulations seemed to anger him the most. But I was well aware that Romanians did not share their personal lives easily, so I never found out why he reacted so strongly.

I found all that he shared with us so fascinating and also disturbing. I wondered how this could happen to a country. How could this one man with almost no schooling gain control over so many? Could this happen in the United States? As I write this in 2022, I'm sorry to say this is no longer a question for me. Our democracy feels a whole lot more fragile than it did in 1992. Then, I felt privileged to be an American, as I do now, but I have lost the sense of security that was either real or imagined in 1992.

At the same time that I felt pride in being an American, I was feeling more at home in Romania. Although not great, my Romanian had improved enough that I was comfortable going to most places and getting what I needed. I understood most of what I heard, but I had a long way to go in speaking the language. When Bill visited at Christmastime, we got an unexpected appointment with Dr. Z. Before entering her office, I warned Bill not to say much out of concern that he would say the wrong thing. We couldn't afford to annoy her. As Bill followed my directions, I heard Dr. Z make fun of him in Romanian to her assistant. She spoke of his long hair and asked if he was dead, not knowing I had told him not to speak. I was so frustrated to understand but not be able to respond. I decided never to attend a meeting without a translator with me. What had I been thinking?

During these winter months of waiting, I became a little more social. I accepted dinner invitations that I might have turned down during my first year in the country because of the language barrier. But now, I enjoyed my evenings out and some good dinners not presented in one pot, the way it was done at Casa. My invitations mainly came from the moms of the bobbies who worked at Casa.

On the whole, Romania felt more like home to me. Bill laughed at me when he visited at Christmas, and we took the train from Bucharest to Constanta. By now, I knew there was little or no heat on the train, so I dressed warmly for our three-hour trip. I had many layers of clothes and, of course, a hat that I rarely took off inside or out. I had warned Bill, but he didn't quite get how cold it could be.

In our train compartment were four of us, two country women and Bill and me. Bill was shivering in the corner of the compartment in his very stylish New York clothes. The two women and I sat warmly with our many layers. What really amused him was when the three of us women pulled out our homemade ham sandwiches simultaneously. When I left the US, I was a vegetarian. Now not only was I eating meat, but I was fitting in. He looked at his wife, who looked like a babushka eating her ham sandwich, alongside the other women. He thought, *Look at her. Oh my God, I have lost her. She has adapted to her environment.*

Part III

Paris, April 1992

I am feeling a little bit like a hobo in my baggy, worn-out jeans, my fuzzy green and blue jacket, and my grungy running shoes. And like a hobo, I don't have any money in my pocket—or at least not enough money for a trip from Romania to Paris. *I sure hope that Bill's at the airport as promised. Otherwise, what will I do?*

These past weeks have been so difficult on every level. It is already April, and I have been back in Romania since August. I am so stuck. Once again, the adoption isn't going anywhere. I am weary; I wonder if it will ever happen. There has been talk in the press that children are being adopted only to be sold. In addition, we are stuck in a catch-22 with both governments. The Romanians are saying that the adoption will be approved when the US approves the children's HIV status. American officials have said that once the children are adopted, they will be approved for entry into the United States. Neither country is willing to take the first step.

I must find a way to get this moving, but I can't see it.

* * *

Sister Julie came for a visit a couple of weeks ago. She could feel my frustration with this process. As

Julie, Marolen, and I were taking a walk one evening by the sea wall, Julie suggested that I scream my anger and frustration out to the Black Sea, which I did. I surprised myself at how deep the feelings went inside of me. The anger tore at my gut until I heard the sound of wailing—a sound I had never heard come from me, the deep pain at the possible loss of my children.

To add to my foul mood for the last week, Rebecca and I had had a bad experience after I went to Bucharest to meet her at the airport. She was the Montessori teacher from California that Starcross had sent over to set up a school at Casa. She was excited and nervous about life in Romania. We got on with each other very well, and after our long trip back to Constanta, we deposited our suitcases at Casa. After dropping the bags, we headed out for a walk so I could show her around town.

On our way back to Casa, we encountered a pack of boys who started to yell names at us, something that I had gotten used to. Some of the kids even liked to try their English out, even though some of the words weren't always appropriate. So I suggested to Rebecca that we ignore them, which usually worked. But this bunch of boys was different. They started to say things I didn't understand about Americans. They became aggressive and began to throw rocks at us and pull at Rebecca. I yelled at them in my broken Romanian and tried to get Rebecca away, but each time I got away, I looked around and saw that they had Rebecca again. They were hurting us, and she wasn't realizing how forceful she had to be with them. I was growing really frightened and frustrated because I wasn't getting through to Rebecca that she was being way too polite with this group of boys.

I'm unsure how we finally got away from them; maybe someone was coming. I don't know. But when we finally got away from them, we were both shaken. I didn't want to say too much about it since Rebecca had just arrived, in fear she might want to catch the next flight out. By the time we got back, we had changed the subject. We were trying to shake it off, only to arrive safely at home to find out that the suitcases we'd left on the balcony had been stolen. I was furious. I'd had enough of Romania.

Brother Toby must have heard how discouraged I was with the adoption. I received a letter from him encouraging me to stay the course and reminding me that even Jesus had been discouraged in his darkest hour when he said to his father, "Why have you forsaken me?" He asked me to have faith. I was touched by Brother Toby's caring letter and appreciated his support. Since being connected with Starcross, I hadn't been aware that my reaction to Christian references had changed. Words and rituals that had brought me a little peace but mostly fear as a child were now feeling more comfortable. This last year, through Starcross, I'd been reintroduced to Christianity. My perspective on it was so different than when I was a child; I saw the peace that it seemed to bring to those who followed and believed. I saw how this group made the doctrine work for them. As I read Brother Toby's words, I found them a bit comforting. I realized that even without my awareness, my spiritual connection had grown. Being part of a religion isn't something I will ever do. But my anger with the church had softened and I appreciated that others could find solace in it.

Along with Brother Toby, Bill was also encouraging me to stay the course. Feeling blue one day, I said to Bill over the crackling phone connection, "I don't know if I can do this anymore. I'm not getting anywhere."

Bill compassionately responded, "Susan, you're not finished yet. Are you?"

Sadly, I agreed. But I said, "I miss you. I wish I could come home." Not even thinking how I could do that.

"How about we meet in Paris for a few days?"

"I wish I could, but I don't have any clothes that I could wear there. I literally have nothing." When I packed to go back to Romania I had never intended to stay so long. The little that I had was worn out and too big from losing weight. And certainly not nice enough for Paris.

"Okay. I dare you to meet me in Paris. Just pack a toothbrush," Bill said, with a smile in his voice. He knew how competitive I could be with him.

"Dare taken," I said, smiling into the phone.

A few days later, feeling like a ragamuffin, I departed Bucharest for Paris on a plane. As I walked into the pristine glare of Charles de Gaulle, I anxiously looked around for Bill, not wanting to think about what I might do if he wasn't there. But in no time at all, I saw him through the crowd of people. Bill looked so handsome. He was wearing one of my favorite looks on him—blue jeans and a sports jacket. His dark auburn hair was long in the back. He looked so happy to see me. His way of looking at me made me feel pretty when just moments ago I had been feeling anything but.

After a long embrace, he gave me the plan: We were going to head over to the Left Bank to buy some new clothes for me. Then we would go to our hotel down the street from Notre Dame and have dinner at a recommended restaurant.

It all sounded so perfect, but it was better than I might have hoped for.

At our first boutique, I felt like Julia Roberts in *Pretty Woman* as my husband and the salesperson dressed me in the latest: tight black pants, a multicolored cowl neck top, and red high-top sneakers. The colors were just what I needed, having worn only dark colors these last months. The best part was the clothes that I'd come in went promptly into the garbage. On our way to our next shop, we stopped for ice cream. In fact, after every two or three shops, we stopped for ice cream. Heaven . . . shop, ice cream, shop, ice cream. To top it all off, Bill brought champagne and chocolate back to our room. I immediately took him up on his goodies. I ran a hot bubble bath, my go-to place for peace and relaxation. I soaked for an hour, and as I did, I ate and drank champagne and chocolate. Life doesn't get much better than that. We didn't make dinner that night.

The next few days were food for my soul. We toured the city, ate great food, and shared the only book in

English we had with us, *The Vampire Diaries*. One of us would read ahead and then tear the pages off the paperback to share with the other. In *The Vampire Diaries*, there are many scenes that take place at Notre Dame, so we visited there a few times as we saw the book come to life. We also wandered the church and its many chapels.

When we came upon the chapel of Joan of Arc, we stopped, feeling a strong connection with her. We prayed to her, directing our energy toward her strong warrior attitude, hoping that she'd give us the strength to continue our fight for the children. Although neither of us had any desire for religion, we still carried an appreciation of the spirit of the soul that the saints represent.

When the day was over, we retired to our cozy room, where each trip to the closet meant we needed to climb over the bed. There was no getting to the closet otherwise. We loved our hotel, though; we found it romantic, of course. Isn't that what Paris is known for?

After three glorious days together, our time had come to an end. I hated to leave Bill, but I was feeling so much better, and I was also surprised that I had started to miss the children. We made a pact with each other not to have a teary goodbye. We left each other with the positive thought that maybe on my return, there would be some good news. After all, it was spring, a time for growth and renewal.

Approval of Romanian Adoption Committee, April 1992

I felt detached. Everyone was so happy all around me. They were congratulating me. I looked inside of myself for a response, but I couldn't seem to find one.

I was standing in the common hallway of Casa Speranta between apartments with Simona, Dr. Matusa, and a few of the Romanian moms that worked for Casa. This area was where we held many of our celebrations, but no matter what we did to fix it up, it never looked good or welcoming. The lack of light and the drab tile floor were depressing. But this is where we celebrated, and clearly, I was the one being honored.

I wondered why I wasn't feeling more elated. Dr. Matusa had just handed me the best news. Dr. Zugravescu had approved our adoption! She and her committee had given permission so we could move ahead. Now all that we needed was the approval of the court.

So why was I not jumping up and down? *This should be easy*, I thought. We had already been before the court three times. The judge had been waiting to hear from the committee for well over a year. I guessed it was all too hard to believe. I decided to look into my strange behavior later; for the moment, I took my lead from the others, and I would celebrate . . . but first, I wanted to call Bill.

"You're going to be a dad," I told him before he'd scarcely said hello.

There was no answer. Did I wake him? I looked at the clock. No. It was noon here, so it was 5 p.m. at home.

"Bill? Are you there?"

"Yes, I'm here."

I could hear the tears in his choked-up voice.

He knew what had happened without me even needing to say. *He's really happy*, I thought. His response allowed me to start to feel the impact of knowing that these four children would be ours. Although this had been my desire for the last year and a half, I never allowed myself to thoroughly take it in.

Now I could really believe that I was Ramona, Ionel, Mihaela, and Loredana's mother.

After my phone call to Bill and more congratulations from the staff and moms, I went in to check on the children. They all looked so angelic as they slept. We had a hard morning. Loredana and Ramona were getting herpes zosters after having had colds. These blisters always made them irritable; they whined all morning. Ionel and Mihaela had been their mischievous selves and, when I was distracted, they took all the clothes out of the wardrobe. By naptime, I was ready to pull my hair out. But as I looked at them with my good news sinking in, my heart opened even more.

Still on a high from the news of the committee's approval, I called my lawyer to see if I could get the court date moved up. My next date was June 15. He said he would find out. He hadn't been even close to good at keeping his word, so I hoped this time he would come through. He later returned with an answer, saying that it wouldn't be possible to move the date up since we were still waiting for the Romanian home study to be completed. So wait again, I did.

* * *

We waited through May and half of June doing what we usually did with the kids. We took walks, went to the beach, and played in the yard. One of the street dogs was nice enough to have her puppies in our yard, in a hole under the sidewalk. Watching and then playing with the puppies led to many hours of enjoyment.

One day while we were playing in the yard, we saw a tractor coming slowly down the street. This was not that unusual; horses and carts and tractors often passed by. But this tractor stopped in front of Casa Speranta. A sturdy, good-looking, dark-haired man climbed down from the tractor. He looked to be in his twenties. As he got closer, I recognized him as Mihaela's father. I knew him and liked him, but I'd had no idea that he was coming, and I wondered what was up.

He told Simona that he was there to see Mihaela.

I loved that he had come to see Mihaela, but he hadn't visited in a long time. I began to wonder if he had changed his mind. Maybe his wife had?

When Bill came to Romania for Christmas, we visited Mihaela's family, and we took Mihaela. I learned that her mother wasn't well; she had some sort of lung problem. As Mihaela was playing, she scraped the paint on the walls. I was apologetic, but the mom told me to leave it. She sadly said that after Mihaela left, she could look at the wall and at least know that she had been there.

The dad and Mihaela sat together on a blanket we had brought out to the yard. He spoke with her so sweetly. She didn't run up to him, nor did she act shy, which she often did with people. She licked the sweet pastry (eating solid food was still a challenge) that he had bought for her. She seemed to enjoy her time with him.

When I asked Mihaela's dad about his wife, he said it was too hard on her to come. It took over two hours on the slow-moving tractor, but I don't think that was what he was referring to. Then he said goodbye to Mihaela, kissed her, and left as quickly as he'd come. That would be the last time that Mihaela would see her father.

* * *

June 15. The day had finally arrived. I felt the excitement like the break of dawn. The sun's entrance in that brief moment can so easily be lost if you're distracted for even a second.

Then the day began. Today was the day I had been waiting for. Today was the day that we would finally get permission from the court. Today, I would return after being in court and say to the kids, "Let's pack our bags; we're going home."

I was nervous and excited. I felt like a caged animal just waiting to break out. Marolen had decided to go with me to lend support, but one of her kids got sick at the last minute, so I had to go alone.

I was to meet the lawyer outside of the courthouse at 3 p.m. My lawyer didn't show up until 3:15, and I was beside myself with worry. But when we got into the courtroom, we were right on time. They had just called our case.

The room was packed with people; it was extremely warm. I felt like I couldn't breathe. I was pushed off to one side. Only my lawyer was allowed to approach the bench. He stood before the judge but didn't give any thought to where I was standing. The courtroom was much like I think of our older courts, with heavy, dark wood and little overhead light. There were a few benches made from dark wood for the lawyers and their clients. The judge's bench sat up high, Judge Judy style. Off to the side, up almost as high as the judge, was someone that I had never noticed before. Like the judge, he wore a wig. I wondered who he was and what he did.

It wasn't long into my lawyer's very brief presentation that this man addressed the court. I didn't understand what was being said, but I noticed that the judge was nodding in agreement. He turned his attention away from my lawyer and gave it solely to the wigged gentleman.

In less than ten minutes, it was over. My lawyer walked up to me and shooed me outside. When we got out into the noisy, crowded, smoky lobby, he told me the news. The wigged man was the prosecuting attorney who was representing the children.

He said, "The prosecuting attorney said that since Costin had gotten better from HIV/AIDS and was returned to his family, these children would also get better under Romania's care. Therefore they should stay in Romania."

"WHAT!" I snapped back at him. "Does this man understand that there is no cure for this disease? That Costin was probably tested wrong in the first place?" I was shouting, my tears and anger building up. "Did he read all my reports and letters from doctors saying that going to America was the best chance the children had to survive? What did you say? How did you defend us?" I demanded.

I could tell from his posture and mumbling words that he had said nothing.

"I've had enough," I said without thinking. "I can't use your services anymore."

This lawyer wasn't doing me any good. I had to do something else.

I cried all the way back to Casa Speranta. I didn't care that the cab driver looked concerned or who else saw my tears. I had no idea what to do now. I was nowhere. The parents had signed the children over to Bill and me. The committee had given their permission, so what could I do now? This wasn't a good place to be; I was terrified. How could I care for the children that had been turned over to me by their families if I couldn't adopt them? This was too much. I felt so alone. I didn't even want to call Bill. I couldn't stand the thought of his disappointment on top of mine.

Simona was almost as upset as I was. Not only was she was concerned for the children and me, but also we'd asked her to come to the US to help with the children. We went to Bucharest and got her visa. She was barely twenty and nervous, never having been away from home. Once she decided to go, she was eager to get on the plane and get going.

Everyone at Casa Speranta was feeling the disappointment and loss I was experiencing. Other volunteers and bobbies were stopping by the apartment to offer their condolences as if someone had died. Unlike times in the past, I couldn't even come up with another plan. I just cried more tears than I thought I had.

When Simona returned to work the following day, she told me her mother's friend was a lawyer, and that she would see if she would help me.

I got to meet with this new lawyer the following week. She was the antithesis of my previous lawyer. She was well dressed, concise, and clear with her instructions for me. I was encouraged when she told me that the judge still had to make his final decision. The next date would be set for July 20. He would look at our file one more time. This was great news. She told me she couldn't guarantee what would happen, but she had a plan.

She went on to say, "I want you to write a letter to the judge. Write this letter from your heart. Tell the judge why you want to adopt these children, children with such a severe illness. Help him to understand." Then she continued, "I know someone who works in his office. She will sneak your letter into his file and put it on top so that it's the first thing he sees when he opens it."

This plan didn't feel like a sure thing, but at least it was something I could do.

Can I do this? I asked myself. Write a letter that my children's health and lives depended on? A letter that could explain how Bill and I felt about them? How could I explain to the judge how I had fought for them over this last year and a half?

This fight was not only legal but physical and emotional as well. There were battles that needed to be fought every day.

It was a daily battle to get Mihaela to nourish herself. At three, she was still refusing to eat without the bottle. Lately, she had started biting everything that wasn't food. In addition, Mihaela also had many doctor visits. We were continually fighting ear infections and swollen adenoids. We knew she needed to have her adenoids removed, but there wasn't a doctor who would operate on her because of fear of HIV infection.

Another physical battle was Loredana, who needed so much, but mostly physical strength. From the day I received her, we'd done physical therapy exercises early every morning to get her to sit upright and bang on a table like a six-month-old. Then she had to do exercises to build strength in her legs. Now, a year and a half later, she was walking. The doctors had told me that this wasn't possible for her.

There were emotional battles that I tried to help the children overcome as they learned to love and trust. How do I explain to the judge how I learned to hold Ionel in the middle of the night when he would wake to such anger and sorrow? That I had learned how slow I had to go with Mihaela to earn her trust? I learned to let her keep her distance from new people, allowing her to observe until she was comfortable. I'd also uncovered and nurtured the part of Loredana that kept her flame alive. It seemed to be by igniting others' spirits through laughter, song, or dance that Loredana came to life. And finally, with Ramona, I had to help her not to fear her overwhelming enthusiasm for life.

In addition, I was battling the pain I felt being separated from Bill and my family because of my love for these children.

I knew that I could never write this letter alone; I needed help. I went to the small room that was our chapel. I sat on the small daybed and looked around. Any space can be sacred if you want it to be. I wanted and needed it to feel sacred now. I felt that way on

Sundays when I did chapel service with the children. If I could feel that way with the children, I could feel it now.

There was a picture of Jesus on the wall. I lost my connection to Jesus when I lost my relationship with the church. I never thought to look at them separately. It never occurred to me that I could take Jesus with me. The power of his spirit struck me. I remembered, as a small child, the comfort I would get when I spoke with him. I thought it all seemed so simple at that moment; leave it to the church to make it complicated. There was also a wooden cross in the room. This cross was from Starcross. They'd told me that it came from fencing, which ran for hundreds of acres in Northern California. The fencing was made from giant redwood trees, and these trees were from the time of Christ. The symbol of the cross does not inspire me, but I did like this one. I liked its simplicity.

On the table with the cross, there were candles. I found the matches and lit them while I asked for help.

I said out loud, "I cannot do this alone. I need help. Please help me."

Then I started to write. I gave the judge some brief information about Bill and me—our years together, marriage, and work. But most importantly, I wanted the judge to know that I came to his country to volunteer; I didn't come to adopt. I fell in love with the children I was caring for. I realized that adoptions had gone terribly wrong for Romania. It was a black mark on the character of the country. I thought it was important that he knew my original intention.

I spoke of Costin and his misleading test. Children were not getting better from this disease. These children had a limited amount of time. But the medical treatment they could get in the US offered them the most longevity. Aside from the medical treatment, we wanted to give the children the family that every child deserves. I wanted him to know that none of these children would ever die alone or among strangers.

I knew that, along with helping the judge to understand, I needed to be brief. From the look of the courtroom, he was a busy man, so I got to the point. I acknowledged that I couldn't rationally explain to him my desire to adopt four children at one time, four children with HIV, whose lives were so uncertain. Children who were not expected to live into their teens.

I told him that there are times in our lives when our hearts can take us to places where our minds would never dare allow us to go. Ours was a decision of the heart . . . my heart and Bill's heart.

Over the years, I have come to refer to this letter as my letter from God. Not only did these words help the judge with his difficult decision, but they have acted as a reminder for me. The words remind me that when I don't have a rational answer it is okay. I have somewhere else to go . . . to my heart.

The heart, when acknowledged: it just knows,
When followed: it is brave

And when allowed: it can expand our world
The heart has an intelligence of its own.

On July 21, 1992, my lawyer delivered the final decision of the court: we were going home.

My Head Is Full of Children,
Part One

We are going home!!! I could now see us, breaking through the clouds together: In my mind's eye, I saw all six of us—Ramona, Ionel, Loredana, Mihaela, Simona, and me—getting on a plane and going home. Romania no longer felt so heavy. As I looked toward the sky, I saw that it was blue and clear. We didn't need to break through; it was open. I wondered how long it had been like that, and I hadn't noticed. Had I been so stuck in my problems that maybe I missed the day that the sky opened for us?

Moving wasn't easy; I didn't know which direction to go first. I had so many thoughts and plans for our return. What did I need for the children on the plane and our time in Bucharest? What food could I travel with for Mihaela, as she still didn't like solid food? *Don't forget to pack toys and books to entertain them,* I told myself. *What clothes shall we bring? I'll need an extra set of clothes for each child to change into right before we get off the plane. Bill will be waiting for us. A transitional item would be good to help them feel secure, maybe their blankets.*

My head was full of children. *Oh, diapers, Pampers,* my mental list went on. I had a dusty Pampers bag under my bed that I'd been saving for this day. Many times I would have loved to use this package of Pampers instead of cloths, but I resisted. I hoped they would still fit. I couldn't be swaddling children on the train and airplane.

I said to myself, almost out loud, *You need to call their birth parents to let them know we're leaving in case they want to come say goodbye.* Ionel's family said they would come overnight by train. We would have all day with them and leave the following day. I wasn't able to connect directly with the other families, but I left messages that we would be leaving.

As soon as possible, I called Bill to tell him the news.

"Bill, we got it! They're ours! The court approved our adoption," I exclaimed.

"That's great, Susan! We're almost there. Do you want to meet me somewhere to celebrate?"

I was confused about his response. Although I was well aware that the Americans still needed to allow our children with HIV/AIDS into the country, I was struck by Bill's less-than-enthusiastic response to my news.

Was he suggesting that we wouldn't be given an exception to the American law? The embassy had given us a verbal promise that as soon as the children were adopted, under Romanian law, we would get this exception. But we didn't have it in hand. This is what I needed to attend to when we went to Bucharest. This was what I left out when speaking with Bill: telling him that I wasn't going to go to Bucharest by myself; we were all going.

The children, Simona, and all our belongings. I was going for it! I realized I was taking a chance. I might get turned down by the embassy for missing a paper, or some official wouldn't allow the exception. But now that the children were ours, I wanted them home. If denied, we might need to turn around and come back to Casa, a three-and-a-half-hour ride. But I would think about that if I needed to. Right now, we were going for it.

"I don't think this is a good time to leave the children," I said, bewildered. Was he having second thoughts, not ready for us? In hindsight, I now see that Bill was expecting this last approval to take time, something he had become accustomed to. I, on the other hand, was mentally on the plane. What wasn't happening was communicating with each other. To add to our struggle to connect, the reception wasn't good. I had to guess at every other word. I hung up the phone feeling incomplete and uneasy and not knowing when I could place another call to him; placing an international call was still a process.

Bill speaks of feeling robotic these last months, like he was operating in a fog. A robot in a fog. He felt like a robot because every day, he was living a solitary life, on hold, going to work, exercising at karate, and going home. Our house no longer had life in it. Everything had stopped. He said even the dog hardly bothered to get up to greet him any longer. The fog around him was his lack of direction; waiting was his mission. Bill had become a master at waiting. This was his mental state when I called him at work.

He said, "If I'd been in a better place, I might have gotten up some energy and got things ready for their return. But I was so used to waiting; it didn't occur to me to get moving."

As far as he was concerned, he had done what he needed to do a long time ago. He bought and put together two bunk beds that beautifully accompanied the dressers and carpets he purchased. There would be two kids sleeping in each room. He agrees if he hadn't been in such a fog when he got the news, he would have purchased a car that we could all fit in. In addition, four car seats, seven bar stools (so the kids could reach the counter to eat), clothes, diapers, toys, and assorted kid stuff. He now wonders if he had any idea what he was getting into.

After getting my call, he just sat at his work desk, finding it difficult to get started again. With the poor connection, it was so hard to understand what I was saying. But he was sure that, as always, nothing was going to happen quickly. Actually, he had started to dread walking into work each morning only to be greeted by, "How's Susan, and what's happening with the kids?" His answer was always the same: "Not much," while hoping that whoever was asking wasn't going to want more details than that. He wasn't going to let me know it, but he had just about run out of patience with this whole process. He didn't even know what that meant; he wasn't going to stop and ask me to come home. But this was pushing him over his limit . . . again, whatever that meant. All he knew for sure was that he really needed movement, something big to happen, to keep him going.

Two Mommies

S till processing my early-morning call to Bill, I stood by the large window in our apartment. It was a warm July day, and the summer sun poured through the window. Simona and I were getting the children dressed in their shorts and sundresses. Standing at the window, I wondered if I would ever miss this place. I noticed that the garbage from our building and the Soviet bloc apartments in the back had been cleaned up. So today, there were no seagulls eating the garbage and no street dogs feasting. The view was looking better than usual. I thought about the many times, looking out this window over the last year and a half, I felt that this day and leaving might never come. I was reminded of one of Brother Toby's favorite haikus, by poet Kobayashi Issa, who died in 1828:

How lovely it is
To look through the broken window
And discover the Milky Way.

I thought of all the days when I needed to look beyond the dirty panes of glass, garbage, rats, and street dogs to see that it was the same sun, moon, and stars in the sky that we shared with Bill in Princeton. I had come to believe it was feeling this connection that would get us home.

As beautiful as today was, it was not easing my tension. We were waiting for a visit from Ionel's family, who had told us they were coming to say goodbye. They were arriving by train from Iasi, but I had no idea what time they would arrive. I was not looking forward to this visit. I had only met his parents a couple of times, and each time I had grown a little fonder of the young couple. My heart was breaking for them having to give up this beautiful three-year-old. I remember Dr. Matusa telling me that they had considered bringing him home but feared that he might not be accepted in their community because of his HIV.

Standing at the window, I wondered how long they would stay and what we would do with them. I was thankful that Simona would be with me to translate. She was my favorite when it came to translating. She was able to translate as words were being said but didn't interrupt and impose her own meaning. She was also gentle and soft-spoken, which was always preferable in this situation.

The family arrived at about 10 a.m. Ionel's father, Georgie, was a tallish, good-looking, dark-haired man. He had a ruddy look from working outside. His mom, Desprina, was also attractive and looked the most like Ionel, with her light hair and brown eyes; Ionel's two older brothers, Daniel and Audi, who were six and eight, also looked like their mom and Ionel. It was awkward being with them. I was now Ionel's mother. They even commented about how his name was now Belfiore. But Desprina was very much his mother also. Who would help him put on his shoes? Hold his hand to cross the street? Get his lunch for him?

The couple told Simona that they would like to go to the beach. I was grateful for this distraction. All ten of us got into taxis that took us a few miles to the Black Sea. We had been there before, and all the children loved it. It was the perfect thing to do to ease the tension.

I found the beach at Mamaia both beautiful and a bit depressing. The ocean and beach are what heals me, having spent so many years with my mother living on the water. The Black Sea filled my need to see the ocean's vastness and be reminded of my place in the world and how small my problems are in relation to the whole. I'd always yearned for some larger powerful waves, like the Atlantic Ocean offers, but this beach still offered the feel of sand under my feet and the smell of salt air. All of this was a comfort to me.

What I found depressing was the surrounding area. Mamaia had been a vacation paradise for all of Europe in the fifties and sixties. It was equal to any resort in the West. In 1971, Ceaușescu decided to pay off the country's national debt and stopped investing in hotels and resorts. The resorts became run-down, and the tourists stopped coming. Now most of the hotels were closed, and the ones that were open had little to offer. This dichotomy of the ocean and beach, backed by the run-down commercial area, left me with a bit of melancholy.

We swam, played ball, built castles, and had superficial conversations. I noticed from time to time that Desprina would go off quietly with her husband. I wondered if she was crying. But when she came back, she showed only a smile.

We finished our day at the beach with pizza and ice cream and then headed back to Casa Speranta. When we returned, we hung around in front of the building, taking pictures and playing with the children. After what felt like a very long time, I asked Simona if I should invite them to come back up to our apartment. She asked them, but they said no.

Simona told me, "They are having a hard time leaving; they don't know how to go."

It was at this point that Desprina picked up Ionel. She was crying as she held him.

Then Ionel turned to me and asked in Romanian, "Mommy crying?"

"Yes," I said in Romanian. And he wiped her tears away.

"She loves you very much, and she is going to miss you," I said.

I wasn't sure how much he really could understand at his age. Then he did something that made me question if it was really happening.

Ionel turned to Desprina and said to her in Romanian, "Mommy hand."

He turned to me and said in English, "Mommy hand."

As he took both our hands, he said, "Two mommies, two mommies' hands."

Just then, I knew I would never forget. I felt that at that moment, this three-year-old joined our hearts together. His moms. I will forever carry her love for him with me, and I have. Over the years, there have been many times when I've looked into his eyes and sent him love, especially from her.

They left soon after that. I promised them that I would do my best to one day bring Ionel to see them. It was a teary goodbye for all of us. After they left, all I wanted to do was get a glass of wine with Marolen. But I wasn't sure how much Ionel had taken on from the emotionally wrenching experience of the day.

I asked him, "Are you okay if I go bye-bye with Marolen?"

He said, "No, stay."

So I stayed, impressed as to how this little guy knew how to care for himself. After about forty-five minutes, he came up to me.

He said, "Mommy, bye bye."

I asked, "You want me to go? It's okay?"

He hugged me and said, "Da."

From time to time, I still think of this young family, such good people, and their loss, and I find it hard to keep a smile on my face.

My Head Is Full of Children, Part Two

We had early-morning train reservations, so we said goodbye to everyone at Casa Speranta the night before. It wasn't a teary goodbye, but a hopeful one. Everyone at Casa wanted a new life for the children. I knew that there was a slight possibility that we might be back if all the paperwork wasn't in order. Marolen and I were the only two people that knew we might return, but like the elephant in the room, we weren't acknowledging it. I had gone over everything repeatedly, but it always seemed that I needed just one more document, stamp, or signature.

I had a meeting set for that day, July 26, with the US embassy consul; I would not feel home free until she approved my documents. As soon as everything was approved, I wanted to get out of the country as quickly as possible. I didn't trust that something couldn't happen that might stop the adoption.

I was packed and ready to go by 6 a.m. We needed to be on the 8 a.m. train to Bucharest. On this particular day, I hadn't been interested in shaking a crib. I wanted the children to sleep as long as possible; we had a long day ahead of us. Simona and I dressed in sundresses. We also put the girls in sundresses and Ionel in shorts. It was going to be a very warm July day. When we got to Bucharest, our first job was to find our apartment for the night. Morgan, the woman whose initial support encouraged us to proceed with the adoption almost two years ago, had arranged for a place for all of us to stay for the night.

Simona's father crammed us and our luggage into his Dacia. The children waved goodbye to Casa Speranta as we headed off to the Constanta train station. It was a little tricky managing a four-year-old, three three-year-olds, and our luggage. I quickly learned a new way of staying on top of the confusion when traveling with the kids. I initiated this plan when we were rushing for the train. I needed to buy tickets, my bag fell open, and my belongings fell out of my purse. I immediately had the children sit in the safest, cleanest place we could find. They were not wandering off, and this way, I could keep my eye on them while I cleaned up my purse and got the tickets. This approach was the first of many times that my children were asked to sit down in strange places so that I could deal with a problem. Simona's father parked the car and helped us on the train with the luggage; we would have to figure out how to deal with the bags when we got to Bucharest. The trip took three hours; we had time to think it through.

Simona and her dad had a teary goodbye; mostly, her dad cried. I think leaving is always the hardest on the one staying behind. To them, life remains the same except for the hole where their dear one resided. The person who is leaving doesn't have the same structure; everything is new. It is harder to miss someone or something that was never there. Simona was his only daughter, so I could appreciate her father's sadness. I wasn't sure how nervous or excited Simona was because the children needed so much attention; it was difficult for us to have a conversation, and Simona is naturally quiet.

A couple of months before, I had asked her if she wanted to come with us to help with the kids. The next day she told me her answer was yes. She applied for a six-month visa and was approved. She would be able to stay with us for six months. Simona never told me how her family felt about her going. Also, she had a boyfriend that I didn't know much about. All I knew was that Simona seemed steadfast in her decision.

The train was a typical European train with compartments. I was happy because I didn't want my excited children, who couldn't sit still, to bother another passenger. I had tried to prepare them for this trip by telling them that we would take a train and an airplane to our new house that had new beds for all of them. They were all excited about having new beds, "big boy and big girl beds." At Casa, they were still in cribs. I knew that they didn't have any sense of what was to come for them. My job was to keep them calm and comfortable for our long journey.

When we got to Bucharest, we managed the bags well enough; there were plenty of baggage carriers around. The overwhelmed children clung tight to our hands, skirts, and carriage as if they were hanging on to a lifeboat; if they let go, they would be lost in a sea of humanity. We caught a cab and found the apartment easily enough. The cab driver didn't even try to cheat me; it must have been the children. It was almost noon when we arrived, so Simona fed the children, and I took off to the embassy. I hoped that we would be able to leave the next day, but I still didn't have airline tickets or the last-minute approval of my documents. I ran through the streets, with the heat of the day starting to rise. When I got to the US embassy, I passed the long line of Romanians waiting to get into the building to apply for a visa. I was allowed immediate access to the building. This treatment made me feel elite, special, and guilty to live in a country that was desired by so many.

When I got inside, I was sweaty from the heat and my nerves. I had a bag with folders full of documents in Romanian and English for the four children and a visa and passport for Simona. If one of the documents were missing, I wouldn't be leaving.

The consul, Virginia White, met with me right away. She couldn't have been nicer. She could see how nervous and hot I was, so she gave me a seat—hard to come by in the embassy—and a glass of water. As lovely as she was, the process took a long time. I was worried about Simona, who was back at the apartment with the four children. What was she doing to keep them content? Did she have enough water and food?

Finally, after about two hours, we were almost ready, but the consul told me the airline agency would be closing shortly, and if I wanted to leave the next day, I had better run over and get my tickets. To help me out, she called ahead to find out if the airlines had any tickets left on the next flight out. They did. They had six business-class tickets to Frankfurt, the last seats left, and then six coach tickets to Newark. "I'll take them," I said. After all this time, if I had a green light to go ahead, I couldn't let the price of the tickets stop me. I would remember to let Bill know about the expected bill. Suddenly I thought, *BILL!!! He has no idea we'll be home tomorrow. I need to call him, but where? How?*

I ran over to get the tickets as Virginia continued to process our papers. When I returned, I almost lost my composure as I explained to Virginia that my husband didn't know I was coming home tomorrow.

Again, she came to my rescue and tried to place a collect call for me. But I was so nervous I forgot Bill's number at work, the number I had been calling for at least ten years. I just couldn't remember it. So after a few failed attempts, I had the call placed to Bill's parents.

"Mom?" I said. "It's Susan."

"Susan? What's the matter?" My mother-in-law always answered the phone with the question, "What's the matter?" She assumed if someone was calling her, something must be wrong.

"I can't remember Bill's number; please tell him we'll be home tomorrow," I said, almost crying. She seemed confused but happy. She said she would and wished me a safe trip.

"Tell him I'll try him from Frankfurt," I said as I ended our call.

As I turned around, I saw the most beautiful sight. On the counter were all my documents piled up: my four books, one for each child, filled with every bit of information about them and us. Police reports, financial reports, references, information about our home and families, and more were included in these books. The embassy was finished. After one and a half years, it was done; I had everything. We were going home! I tried to let it sink in, but I understood it would take time, and at that moment, I didn't have time. Simona had been alone in a strange place with the children for almost six hours.

I thanked everyone who had helped me, especially Consul Virginia White. As I left the building, I felt proud to be an American. *Americans know how to get things done and done quickly,* I thought.

When I returned to the apartment, I found Simona looking a bit frazzled, but the kids were in good shape. It was almost 6 p.m. They had been in the apartment since 11:30 with only a very short nap. Simona and I gathered the kids and got them out for food and a run in the park. Then it was back to the apartment for a bath and bed. We had an 8 a.m. flight to Frankfurt, which meant we needed to leave the apartment at 5 a.m. We arranged a car to drive us to the airport.

Surprisingly, the children went to sleep easily. Aside from their cribs, they had never slept anywhere else, but they were doing great on all levels. I now recognized each of the children's stress patterns. Ramona, when under stress, talked constantly. It didn't matter if it was Romanian, English, or babble. She didn't care. Ionel shook his hands in front of him as if he wanted to shake off the stress. Mihaela would rub her tongue against her teeth, separate herself, and get even quieter than usual when stressed. And when life was too much for Loredana, she would have a tantrum by throwing herself back and holding her breath. We had seen a few of these patterns today, but on the whole, they were doing great.

Foggy-headed from the early morning, Simona and I got the kids and ourselves ready for our 5 a.m. trip to the airport. The man who picked us up was the same person whose apartment we had rented for the night. Since it wasn't an official cab, I had to do the Romanian money dance with him about how much I should pay.

"How much do I owe you?"

"Whatever you think."

Ugh! At 5 a.m., I had no patience for this. If I gave too little, I would insult him. And normally, if I gave too much, I would feel cheated. But I wasn't staying, so what did I care? I gave him a lot, and it was in dollars. Dollars made it worth even more.

We could check in for our flight at 6 a.m. and were right on time. We got the children all set with some extra drinks and biscuits "just in case." Then we headed over to immigration for one more stop before being free to leave the country. I handed the official our papers; he raised his head to look at who was taking four children home. Then he looked over at Simona and the children. I am sure he'd seen a lot with all the children adopted from Romania, but from the look on his face, he hadn't seen this one before. He didn't look like he liked it. He reminded me of a clerk in Constanta who needed to put stamps on a document for me. She was angry. She told my translator she thought the child was being sold. Her manner only softened a bit when the translator told her the child was sick and needed medication. She said she understood but still didn't agree. This immigration official had a similar look to him as he went through my papers.

At the embassy, they had put together the papers I would be asked for at immigration. So I'd packed all my books of documents in our suitcases. As he looked over the documents, suddenly, he had a look of "gotcha" on his face. He asked me for a paper I didn't have, but I knew exactly where it was. It was in my suitcase, and I could get it. All of our suitcases were no more than ten feet away, waiting to be loaded onto the plane.

"I will get it. It is just over there," I pointed to my suitcases.

"No!" He nearly shouted. "*Nu este voie*. It is not allowed." He called for his superior, and a lot of conversation that I didn't understand ensued. I kept pointing to my suitcases, telling them they were only a few feet away.

At this point, the children were getting impatient. Simona and I kept trying to herd them back in place because if they passed the immigration officer, they would be out of the country. And as far as I was concerned, there was no going back, not even an inch. So I sat them down on the floor in this small passageway that led passengers through immigration. I took out some bananas and, despite the officials' disdain, gave them to the children while we waited. I wasn't sure what we were waiting for, but as long as a conversation was going on, I believed something was happening.

Passengers going through immigration needed to walk carefully so as not to step on the children. It was primarily businessmen on this early flight. At one point, the top official said something to Simona about the children. I heard her raise her voice and say something back. He raised his voice again and spoke about the frontier, that the children could not cross the frontier. She was tired and nervous, and this man was being just rude enough to bring her to tears. Now I was getting worried. When I asked Simona to find out what was going on, all she could report was that they said they were working on it. No one would say how or when we might have an answer. This was not the first time in the adoption process that I had come across this kind of withholding of information; in fact, it was quite common. I suspect it came from living under a communist regime when the Securitate was thought to be everywhere.

It was close to our plane's departure time and nothing was happening; conversation at the desk had stopped. All the businessmen had boarded the plane. The kids weren't happy sitting on the floor any longer. I didn't know what to do. Now I was close to tears. I thought, *I can't go back; I'm too close. I'm only a few hundred feet away from getting on the plane. Maybe I should call the embassy.*

Just then, the man who had stopped us called me to his station and, without looking up—a sign of his disapproval—handed me our passports and told us to go ahead. I got the kids up and stuffed the banana peels into my bag; there was no time to find the garbage. We rushed across the line they called the frontier and onto the plane. On the plane, we turned left into business class. I'm sure this had been the businessmen's fear: the kids they'd needed to step over were sharing a cabin with them. Small, tired children were probably not the way they wanted to start a business trip. Another time, I would have been sensitive to their concern, but I didn't care one bit at that moment.

The plane took off, and a few tears rolled down my face. I couldn't allow too many tears because I didn't want to upset the kids. There were many more tears I held inside. As we cleared Romanian airspace, I breathed a sigh of relief, but my body was still tight from the stress of the morning. My head knew it was safe to relax, but my body hadn't gotten the message. Looking around at my family, I could see that some of the children were unsure, so I put my feelings aside for the time being.

Now it was on to Frankfurt and home, nine hours of flying time and three hours of layover in Frankfurt.

Our layover went as well as expected, with four kids and two tired, stressed-out caretakers. We had a few meltdowns but nothing that bad. I placed a collect call to Bill, who was still laughing that I couldn't remember his phone number. He said he would be at the airport to meet us. Later that day, he confessed that when he heard from his mom we would arrive the next day, he broke out in a cold sweat and thought to himself, *What have I done?*

Our last leg of the trip home was pretty good. The children didn't sleep as much as I had hoped but stayed quiet. That is, everyone but Ramona, who was wearing my ears out with her incessant talking. I must have looked exhausted at one point because a couple of the flight attendants took the children for a while.

As we started to land in Newark, I looked out the window and knew I would never look at this airport the same way I had in the past. I was home. I was an American. I was a mom.

The flight crew told us that after the plane landed, we would need to wait because someone was coming to escort us. I didn't know what that was about; maybe Bill had sent someone to help us. So we waited until we were the last ones on the plane. Then a lovely, elderly man came to show us the way and help us with our baggage. It seemed that he was a porter. But who had arranged for him? He waited as we went through cus-toms, brought us to a private room to go through immi-gration, and waited with us again. No one was saying what was up; he didn't seem to know because he asked me if I knew. Then suddenly, it became clear to me. I remembered filling out paperwork that stated that Newark was our port of entry to the US. We were being detained because the children had HIV. The entry of anyone to the US who had HIV was still against the law. The kids had been given a special exception, but they were being tracked. It began to sink in that HIV was going to be a day-to-day issue in the US, unlike in Romania, where we'd spent every day in a building with thirty children who had HIV. At Casa, no one thought much about how to deal with it; we knew. Now in the States, we would be starting all over again to bring awareness.

The immigration process took over an hour, and there was no way to let Bill know we were okay and had been on the plane. After the children's photos were taken and green cards issued, the elderly man in charge of us led us out and down the hall. The kids walked and were carried as necessary. We went quite a ways with him and then through a self-opening door, and all of a sudden, the man was gone. *Where did he go?* I wondered. I was really disappointed; I'd wanted to thank him and tip him. He had been so nice to us. But he was gone.

We continued down another dimly lit hallway for what seemed like a long way and a long time. My anticipation of seeing Bill was so high it magnified the distance with each step. We caught glimpses of light and noise as the people before us moved through a door ahead of us. Then it was our turn. We went through another set of self-opening doors that thrust us into the noise and lights of the greeting area as if giving birth to our new family.

There was Bill. He looked so handsome in his blazer and jeans, so excited with his arms wide open to greet his family. There he was, the force that pulled us home, the force that never wavered for these last two years in his love for me and his mission to adopt these children. We embraced with Ionel hanging onto my skirt and Loredana in my arms. I thought to myself, *Take this in! You've worked so hard and waited so long for this moment. This moment you will never forget.*

But as much as I tried, it was too much to take in all at once. The images around me were overwhelming. Bill hugged the children. One, two, three, four, and Simona five, yes, they were all there. Hugging Bill's mom and dad. My friends were off to the side just waiting to see me and meet the children. My brother-in-law, his wife, and their children were there; the children were going to meet their cousins. Balloons, my niece, a friend with a video . . . more friends. Is Simona okay? One, two, three, four, and Simona. Yes, all accounted for. Pictures. More hugs. Where's Mihaela? Hiding behind Simona. It's a lot for her. Oops, Ionel is riding on the baggage carousel. Ramona is hugging and kissing Alex, her four-year-old cousin. HIV . . . is my sister-in-law going to be concerned ... more hugs ... Loredana in my friend's arms ... too much to take in. Where is Bill? I need to feel him by my side.

Bill let me know that there was a limo outside waiting for us. I made a face about being extravagant as he reminded me that we didn't have a vehicle big enough to hold all of us now; with Simona, we had a family of seven.

Home

We headed off in our extra-long limo down the New Jersey Turnpike. There were nine of us in the car: two friends; Simona, Bill, and I; and the four children. The children were exhausted but too excited to allow themselves to close their eyes for the hour-long ride home. Only when we were just a couple of miles from home could Ionel no longer fight his tiredness and finally fell asleep in my friend Susan's arms. The three girls were still wide awake, talking about seeing their new beds. Ramona was trying out her use of the word *tata*, which had Bill grinning with delight. We had come to the United States with a vocabulary no one understood. To help the children if the adoption didn't go through, I hadn't wanted to leave them with just English. So in the same sentence, we would use Romanian and English words. Look, *acola*, look there. No one knew what we were saying.

As we drove down the long driveway to the house, I saw bouquets of balloons welcoming us home. Tears of joy filled my eyes, only to suddenly be replaced by a feeling of being overwhelmed. The emotions were too strong. I would feel them for a moment and then feel numb. I saw the girls scrambling out of the car, running to get the balloons, as Ionel was carried up the pathway asleep in Susan's arms. Just then, Falkor ran out to see what was up, scaring the children for the next month. In his puppy-like behavior of jumping and playing, he knocked the toddlers over, so for the following weeks, when he was in the house, they were out, and vice versa.

"We're home!" I announced to Bill as I entered the house, Mihaela and Loredana tight by my side. The girls were just over their scare from the dog and not sure what might pop out next. Ionel was now awake, and Susan was showing Simona, Ramona, and Ionel around the house. They insisted on being shown their new beds. To give the children something to relate to through this journey, I had told them that we were going to a new home with new beds. I knew that this was something they would understand. To get the idea across one evening at Casa, we pretended with blocks on the floor to build our new house. We had two bedrooms, and we all decided who would sleep together by whichever two happened to be paired up that day. Ramona and Ionel were together, and Mihaela and Loredana. The children traded playmates every few days. I don't know how it was decided; I wasn't part of that group, and therefore not privy to that information. It was something that came easily to them without fighting, so I didn't get involved.

So when we all climbed the stairs to their new rooms, they remembered who had gone together. At the top of the stairs was a small passageway between two small bedrooms that shared a bathroom. As I entered the first room, I was overcome by what Bill had done with it. There was a beautiful, brilliant red bunk bed with specially made red and blue rainbow quilts. The walls had been painted by a friend of mine with little animals here and there. On the wall over the beds was a large bird with a rainbow for a tail, the length of the wall. On each bed hung new pajamas for Ionel and Ramona; this was their room. They were as excited as I was as they jumped on their new beds, saying, "Mommy bed, Mommy bed!" Ionel quickly found a truck on his new matching red and white dresser. He then started to exclaim, "Mommy truck, Mommy truck!" The matching carpet, the new clothes in the closet, and all the accessories—Bill had done so much. I didn't have words that could do any better than the hugs I gave him.

Now I was being pulled by another pair of excited hands. Mihaela was dragging me across to her room. Again I was overcome by the transformation of this room. The room had a shiny white bunk bed with quilts in lavender and white. Mihaela and Loredana were already jumping up and down and climbing up the ladder. "Mommy, look!" That is what I heard as they showed me their jumping tricks. The room had cute cartoon drawings of squirrels and deer on the wall. There was a white and lavender dresser and a white carpet with lavender flowers. The room was perfect, with the added touch of new pajamas hanging from the beds. This was all more than I could have hoped for them. As we watched the children, Bill and I looked at each other. I saw how much he was loving the noise and enthusiasm of the children.

Bill had given them the best of everything. We stayed in their rooms for a long time as the kids had us try their new beds out with them. It wasn't enough to have one of us try; we both had to try each child's bed. Then it was Simona's turn, and our friends, Jackie and Susan's. Finally, we were allowed to continue to the rest of the house.

We showed Simona her room, which was downstairs, off the kitchen. It was a room that we had used as an office. Bill had newly redecorated this room also. On her bed was a beautifully wrapped package welcoming her here; inside was a printed silky bathrobe. She was pretty thrilled with her room and her gift. She said, "Everything is so beautiful." She was amazed to see our old but huge Garland stove in the kitchen. I knew she was overwhelmed because I was and it was my house.

I didn't understand how the kids were still standing up by this time. So Simona and I fed, bathed, and got them into bed while Bill unpacked us. Simona said, "I'll stay with them until they go to sleep. Go spend some time with Bill." This was the first of many nights that she would do this since the kids were no longer in cribs, making it easy to escape from bed.

Bill and I kissed and hugged each child good night. I gave them each their transitional blanket from Romania, but no one was interested in it. They didn't seem to be having any problem with the move.

"Good night, Ramona; we love you. Welcome to your new home," I whispered to her.

"Good night," I said to Ionel, who was in the bunk under Ramona. "I love you so much."

As I crossed the small area connecting the children's rooms, I had a brief thought. *I can't lose them.* Then as quickly as that thought came, I choked it down with the voice that said, *Don't go there, not tonight.*

Pulling the covers up on Mihaela, I said, "Good night, Mihaela. I love you so much."

"Good night, Loredana, we love you. See you in the morning. We have a lot to do tomorrow," I said as I kissed and hugged her.

Our busy, somewhat chaotic house was now peaceful and quiet. Bill and I sat on the living room couch with the dog at our feet, as we had just two years before. Since it was quiet now, we could hear the sound of the crickets. I made a mental note to show the children lightning bugs and show them how to catch them. But unlike two years ago, we had no desire to lose ourselves in TV. I didn't want to get lost in anything. I wanted to be present. Finally, the people that I loved the most in this world were all together. I no longer needed to be without one to have the other.

I said to Bill, "I don't want to take any of this for granted. I want to experience every moment with our children. I am feeling so blessed. I never want to forget this moment."

With a smirk on his face, Bill responded, "I feel the same way—I can't wait until morning to see the kids in their PJs, coming down for breakfast. I want to make pancakes the way my dad used to do." Then I saw where the smirk was taking him as he interjected, "And anyway, you're not allowed to watch TV anymore; look what you got us into."

Life in Princeton,
Extraordinary to Ordinary

Our life with the children was all that we had hoped. The children loved meeting new people and traveling. We went to Puerto Rico, Florida, London, and Ireland in their first five years. We also took them to Disney World, although we knew that the kids weren't ready. Later Bill and I admitted to ourselves that it was probably more for us that we went. We were eager to see the children's response to the park and the characters, but we quickly learned that the children were afraid of loud and dark, and Disney exhibits are loud and dark. A few years later, we gave Disney another try, but it proved not to be a vacation for us.

There were so many other fun things to do with the children. The ordinary felt extraordinary when we were with them. One of those ordinary moments I will never forget is when we took the children to the battlefield in Princeton. The field is two large open spaces of grass on either side of the road. You can easily visualize the two opposing armies, the British on one side and the colonists on the other, lined up, ready to shoot.

Only one massive, old oak tree stood in the middle of one side of the field. The children, Bill, and I had fun under that tree all morning, playing soccer, flying kites, and playing frisbee with the dog.

I brought lunch, so we spread out the blankets and ate our peanut butter and jelly sandwiches—a very American lunch for some very newly American kids. Then, as has happened many times and in many places since, I said to the children, "It's time to take a nap." Sometimes, I promised them sleep and then ice cream to make my request more enticing. But this day, it wasn't necessary; the children were exhausted. Naps are Bill's specialty, so he was already asleep, and so was Falkor. The warm fall day was quickly making the children sleepy. One by one, they drifted off to sleep. As I sat and watched my family sleeping on the blanket in front of me, I said to myself, *This moment is perfect. Store this picture, Susan; this is what you have created.* I loved that this was my moment. I was all alone with my experience. Unlike at our arrival at the airport, I had no one else to look after; I could just appreciate this time. All I wanted to do was drink up the beauty of my family and the feeling of gratitude. At this moment, life was perfect.

The children all had medical needs that were extremely time-consuming. They saw the pediatrician, infectious disease specialist, homeopath, and nutritionist and had bloodwork done every three months. Doctor visits with our group were outings, often taking most of the day. To help us out, sometimes our pediatrician would come outside into the yard where the children were playing to examine them. He knew how hard it was for them to have a long wait in his tiny waiting room.

When we went to the infectious disease specialist, a friend would always clear her calendar and come with us. We needed to go to Newark, about an hour's drive. Once we got there, it was always a long wait at the doctor's office just to be seen. Then multiply that wait time by four. Our experience of everything we did was to multiply it times four. But with the help of our friend, Ellyn, the children always had fun playing with the toys and games. We even had a special area in the hospital when getting bloodwork. It was a back corner near the lab where the kids could stretch out on the floor to play with their toys. The nurses knew where to go to find the Belfiore kids. After bloodwork, if the blood draws had been difficult, we would stop for a "silly" breakfast, ice cream at 8 a.m., and then head off to school.

At home, the children's medical needs took priority. Every three months after bloodwork, I would speak to Nick Siano, who wrote the book *No Time to Wait* about the benefits of watching the bloodwork and responding to the virus with supplements before it manifests outwardly. Nick was connected with the newly formed Buyers Club and therefore had the latest info on HIV and AIDS. I will never know precisely how effective the many supplements (approximately ten for each child three times a day) were, but it made me feel that at least I was doing something to keep them healthy when there was nothing else to offer. Unfortunately, there was no medication to stop the virus at that time. At our first appointment with our infectious disease specialist, the children were put on AZT. They took the drug for about a month—then I read that adults taking AZT alone were dying faster than those taking nothing.

Do I take the children off the medication or keep them on? This choice was probably one of the hardest I had had to make with the children's lives so far. What if I decided to take them off the drug, and one or more of them got sick and didn't survive? How would I live with that decision? Or, if I gave them the medication, what would it do to their systems? Since there was no clear answer, I went with my gut. I took them off. But, differently than I might have done for myself in the past, I asked for the support of their doctor with my decision. My way for myself would have been not to tell anyone I wasn't taking it. I was so glad to have done it correctly, because I got their doctor's support. He told me, "Mrs. Belfiore, you have my support. We have no answers for this virus; at this point, we are only guessing."

We went many years without following the protocol for treating children with HIV. It then became apparent that Mihaela was going to need something. She had started to pick up opportunistic infections: ear infections, shingles, herpes zosters, and pneumonia. She was losing weight and had no appetite.

We were so blessed because exactly when she needed medication, a new class of drugs became available to her. It was a protease inhibitor, a cocktail of drugs that would attack the virus at different stages. These drugs were good; in many cases, they changed the face of the virus from a deadly disease to a more manageable condition. Loredana would follow shortly after Mihaela in starting this medication. Both the girls are still on a form of this medication today. And Ramona and Ionel are still medication-free. I always felt so blessed to have doctors who treated my children as individuals and trusted themselves and me to use the protocol as a guideline instead of a mandate.

The day we started Mihaela on her first medication, which she would, in some form or another, be taking for the rest of her life, we all put on silly hats. We decided that this was a good night for an impromptu party. We took the medication from the medicine bottle and put it into a box with horses on it. Mihaela's love is horses. Then it was time for ice cream, sprinkles, balloons, and songs. In my mind, I blessed the medication and accepted it into our lives.

Not All Fun and Games

Although their medical treatment was a challenge, with the wrong decision possibly leading to an irreconcilable outcome, their medical life didn't have the day-to-day pressure and worry that school brought with it. Every day I lived with the stress of having children with HIV in school. In retrospect, I can see that it was the fear of rejection. Since our first child entered school, I feared they wouldn't be accepted. In 1993 and 1994, there was still a lot of misinformation and fear in the general public regarding HIV/AIDS. I was never afraid of the children passing the virus on to another child; it's not easy to catch. My fear was having our children rejected by their peers.

One of the first children to be public about having the disease, Ryan White, had had a bullet shot into his house when he entered the school system just a few years prior. Anytime I would register a child for school, camp, or extracurricular classes, I always told the person in charge about my child's HIV status. There was never a time when someone with them didn't know about them having the disease. Universal precautions were becoming standard practice, and the law didn't require me to reveal their status. Regardless, disclosing felt right to me. Actually, it felt right and wrong at the same time. Right, because I wanted everyone to be safe. Right, because if our family didn't speak about the virus, how would the fear and prejudice around it ever end? Wrong, because it made people feel uncomfortable. I never knew how the information would be received. I came to learn not to trust someone's initial response, whether it was positive or negative. People needed time to process how they felt. They needed to learn about the virus and speak with their loved ones.

Although I feared having the children rejected, I was only aware of it happening a few times. Once was when Ionel went to kindergarten. He was attending a private school in the Princeton area. We were excited to have him attend there since the school went through eighth grade. Early in the year, he was invited to a birthday party. When I told the mom he had HIV, he was disinvited from the party. This led to parents talking and their fear rising. I think the children were given information from the parents because Ionel started to feel uncomfortable at school. He would get carsick every day on his way to school, and to add to the discomfort, Ionel bit a girl on her hand while playing dinosaurs. I was sick about it. He had given the parents something to validate their fear. I knew fixing this would take more than a conversation if Ionel were to remain at this school. Together with the administration, we called a meeting for all the kindergarten parents, about forty families. I asked the children's infectious disease specialist to speak. In the days leading up to the meeting, I was terrified. Before we left for school on the evening of the discussion, Bill and I took the time to ask God for help. We felt like an assembly room filled with angry kindergarten parents was more than we could handle ourselves.

Our family meeting did not go well; kindergarten parents are not easy. Bill and I overheard a couple who didn't recognize us say to each other, "What, did they think they were going to get away with this; keep it a secret?" They had no idea that I was the one who'd told the school that Ionel had the virus.

To the assembly, I spoke about the history of our adoption. The principal addressed how we had been upfront and the guidelines he needed to follow, and then the infectious disease specialist answered questions. But it was obvious that this group of parents had not been convinced that it was safe to have a child with HIV in school. They wanted our son out. It took me years to realize that the parents needed reassurance from me that evening. They needed my assurance that it was safe to be with someone who had HIV. Instead, my fear of our family being rejected was what the parents got from me. It was not until I realized this that I could let go of feeling like our family had been the victims.

Over the next week, Ionel felt worse every day about school. So finally, I decided to take him out and put him in a small school the girls were attending. I felt like I was running, and I guess I was, but Ionel was only five years old. I couldn't put him in an environment where he wasn't wanted.

Today I can still feel the pain that I experienced during that time. I tried so hard never to let Ionel know what was going on. So I faced loneliness and rejection for him. I tend to like to please people, but I wasn't pleasing anyone. I spent many days feeling like I had done something wrong. I had brought something to the school that the kindergarten parents didn't want to face. As one man said, "This was why I sent my son to private school. He shouldn't be exposed to this kind of thing here."

As the years went by, we had one or two other times when the children's health was a big issue. I learned years after the fact that our contractor ran into a problem when remodeling our home. The carpenters assigned to our project heard of our children's health and refused to start work. Our contractor, who later became our good friend, got a professional to educate the guys about the virus, giving them the comfort level they needed to start. By the end of the job, the guys were all playing with the kids. My friend never told me what she went through to get the project started. I have a photo on my wall of her showing the kids how to hammer. It was only after hearing about what happened that I realized she wasn't just showing my kids how to hammer; she was setting an example for the carpenters that they didn't need to be afraid.

Another time, an audiologist refused to give my daughter a hearing test because she did not want to put headphones on her. She was concerned because she wanted to get pregnant shortly. This misinformed person should not have been in the health field.

These misconceptions about the virus showed us how large the need was for people to learn about the disease and advocate for those who had the virus. We realized that meant us. How could we expect anyone else to speak out if we didn't speak up? As soon as we made that decision, the doorway of opportunity opened.

Primetime Live had been following Brother Toby and the Romanian/HIV story since Brother Toby's first trip to Romania. They asked us to do a follow-up story covering the children's entrance to the United States and their new family life. The show was the perfect opportunity to show people that there was no need to fear those who had the virus.

When ABC's producer showed up and got in a pile of leaves and had a leaf fight with the kids, I thought to myself, *This is who I want to tell our story*. She didn't seem nervous being with the children; she acted comfortable. I was nervous until the program aired, but it was a truthful, honest piece on our family. From the feedback we got, I believe it accomplished what we wanted: to put a face on this virus and teach people that they didn't need to fear those who had the disease. Our story helped bring attention to the stigma and discrimination associated with HIV. We felt so comfortable with the correspondent and the producers that we did two more pieces with them over ten years.

After this first piece aired, Bill, the children, and I opened ourselves to spreading awareness as best we could. We did interviews with newspapers, books, and magazines about our family. We all did speaking events. Ionel, at age twelve, spoke at the International AIDS Conference in Toronto, and Ramona and Ionel spoke at several universities. We all found the same thing: the closer we got to home and the more involved with the group we were, the more nervous we got to speak. Our children all spoke with their high schools about HIV; they are so brave.

I needed direction when I was looking for a way to address the parents at Ionel's school. I came across an organization, the Elizabeth Glaser Pediatric AIDS Foundation, with information on exactly how to go about my presentation. The information was from when Elizabeth spoke with her child's school. Elizabeth herself was infected with the AIDS virus from a transfusion and unknowingly passed it on at birth to her children. Before she died, she started the Pediatric AIDS Foundation and brought awareness to the needs of those infected by speaking out at the 1992 Democratic National Convention.

Bill joined the board of the Elizabeth Glaser Pediatric AIDS Foundation. Their mission was to stop mother-to-child transmission and raise money for AIDS research. Also, we were involved in helping this organization get a bill passed in Congress that would require drug companies to test their products for use in children before coming to market. At that time, over 80 percent of all medication had never been tested for children. The lack of testing directly affected us when Mihaela came off her new medication because she developed a resistance to the drug. She should have been taking more; it had not been tested for use in children. I testified to this before the House and the Senate. As a result, the Pediatric Rule was passed by a bipartisan committee and signed into law by George W. Bush.

Our association with the Pediatric AIDS Foundation positively affected the children, who faced discrimination daily from the disease. They would go from being alienated at school to feeling like superstars at the foundation's events. Hundreds of caring people attended their fundraising events. Movie stars donated their time to raise money for research. Our kids felt so cool, having met Tom Cruise, Justin Timberlake, Penelope Cruz, Seth Green, Magic Johnson, and many more celebrities. Knowing that all these people were stepping up to help them gave them the courage to face their lives back home.

Again with the Pediatric AIDS Foundation, we traveled to Africa to participate in AIDS walks. Bill and I took turns going and bringing a different child with us each year. Our trips to Africa led us through impoverished villages in Soweto, Tanzania, South Africa, and Swaziland. We visited schools and helped them paint and do light construction. We also visited hospitals and learned how they were dealing with the virus. Our children stayed away from going into the hospitals because it upset them. Bill and I supported their decision. Even without entering the hospitals, the children's presence and health gave hope to those infected. When Ramona was visiting a school in Tanzania, a man followed her. Bill asked someone to see what this seemingly good-natured man wanted. The man said, "I cannot believe that this girl is twelve years old. We have never seen a child with AIDS this old."

Our purpose in doing these trips was to raise funds, bring hope to Africa, and bring awareness of Africa's needs back to the United States.

Brother Toby had also gotten involved in Africa, helping children who had contracted HIV. My favorite story from one of his trips was about a young girl who asked him to tell her about the children in the US. She said to him, "Brother Toby, tell me about the children in the US. Do they sing and dance every day as we do?" He answered, "No, they don't." The little girl responded, "Oh, I feel so sorry for them." This attitude was the most significant takeaway from our trips to Africa. We were all moved by how joyful the people were, singing and dancing at a moment's notice. Each trip would help our family to reconnect with our blessings.

If anything came out of our being so public about the virus, it was that each time we spoke about our experience, our words would always bring us back to our blessings. Mihaela said it beautifully when our family spoke to an audience at Tavern on the Green for World AIDS Day. She said, "Without HIV/AIDS, I wouldn't have the family that I have today."

Aidan Joseph

On December 13, 1995, our fifth child entered the world! Aidan Joseph was born to us after twenty-four years of marriage and when I was forty-five. As Bill and I often say, God has a strange sense of humor.

I had not been feeling well but assumed I had entered menopause. I had gone to the doctor, chiropractor, and nutritionist to alleviate my discomfort. One day I found myself drinking flat ginger ale and eating saltines in an attempt to feel better. *This is strange*, I said to myself. *This is what a pregnant woman might do.* I took an at-home pregnancy test. It was positive. Confused, I didn't know what to do. I paced back and forth across the bedroom. I thought, *Do I call Bill? How can I tell him that over the phone when he's on the trading desk? Do I call [my good friend] Karen? I can't tell a friend before Bill. Wait. First, I better call the doctor to make sure this test is correct.*

When I called the doctor's office, the nurse told me that the at-home kits were accurate. I said, "But you don't understand. I'm forty-five years old. I have never conceived in my twenty years of marriage—oh, and by the way, we just adopted four children at once. I can't be pregnant." The very patient nurse understood my dilemma and told me to come in, and they would do a blood test. So now I thought, *Do I call Bill now or wait until I know for sure? I have to let him know because, along with being my husband, he's my best friend, and I need to tell someone.*

The doctor never did the bloodwork. Instead, I went in a matter of hours from thinking I was in menopause to seeing our three-month-old baby in utero. When I got out to the car from the doctor's office, I called Bill right away.

"Bill Belfiore, please," I asked the voice that picked up.

I thought, *I'd like to wait until he gets home, but I've already alerted him, and it's been almost twenty-five years of waiting . . . I'm calling.*

"Bill, I'm pregnant," I said when he answered the phone.

"You are? Are you sure?"

"Yes, I saw the baby. I have pictures," I quietly answered, not knowing what he was thinking. This was not the response I was expecting. But I really didn't know what to expect from him because *I* didn't know what to think. Yes, I'd always wanted to give birth, even though for most of my married life, I didn't acknowledge it. But now? At forty-five? We had just started our family with four children. I felt happy and confused. I realized what I wanted from Bill was what he couldn't give me: a definite reaction. He was as thrown by the news as I was.

"*Now* you get pregnant, after all this time?" he asked. "I guess we'll talk about it later."

"Okay," I answered, knowing it wasn't easy to speak while working on the desk. He told me later that week that it took days for the information to settle in.

When Bill returned home from work that evening, he didn't say much. What he did was to start to clean things that didn't need cleaning. He started the wash. I followed him around, waiting for his response, until finally I said, "Don't you think we should talk about this?" We sat down together, but we both had little to say.

My pregnancy went very well. Our families and friends were almost as thrilled as we were. The kids couldn't wait to have a new brother. We found out it was a boy not long after we found out we were expecting. The children attended a class at the hospital on how babies are born. So, for the last few months of my pregnancy, four big pictures that the children made of babies in utero were hanging in the kitchen.

Aidan was a good size baby, at 8 pounds, 11 ounces. He seemed to be born with an appetite. When the nurses handed him to me, they said, "Watch out, he's a piranha."

And he was. When he was hungry, there was no denying him for even a few minutes. The children were thrilled to have a new baby—well, most of the time. After a few months, Loredana, whom Aidan displaced as the smallest, complained about him. When I reminded her that she had wanted a baby, she responded, "I did, but I didn't know he was going to stay."

Aidan was born to a large family and a busy house.

On his first day in the world, he was greeted by forty-five people, friends and family, who came to the hospital to meet and hold him. His birth was celebrated like Simba's in *The Lion King*. We had so many gifts coming into the house I had to take a break from opening them. The UPS driver was at our house so often he became like family.

Aidan had a big job on this earth, and he started his work immediately. At least one of his purposes was to get us to be experienced as a typical family. Up until his birth, our family was not seen as typical; we were either viewed with fear or admired for adopting HIV-positive children. Our lives were covered by newspapers, magazines, and television. On the flip side of the positive coverage was our children's lack of play-dates and friends. It was a constant issue. We never allowed our children to go anywhere without someone knowing about their health; that meant constantly revealing their status and waiting to see the response.

Aidan's birth marked the start of our family's first day with this new identity. We would no longer see ourselves or be seen as just the HIV/AIDS family, as we had for those first few years. Often when parents were afraid to let their child play with one of ours, they would refer to the fact that all our children had the virus. We were not exposing a healthy child to those that carried the virus. They were right, and although I felt it was safe, I couldn't speak from experience. Now that we had Aidan, I could sincerely say I felt completely safe with him being with the other children. Not one day did I ever fear for his safety. By the time Aidan was born, Bill and I had lived with HIV for at least five years. I had been with kids that had full-blown AIDS and those who were very healthy. I had learned that either way the virus wasn't easily transmitted. As Bill said, "This was just how we lived our lives. For ourselves, we no longer gave it any special thought."

A Gift

Almost two years prior to Aidan's birth, my father-in-law called me over to his side. He was sitting on our couch, bent over, taking in oxygen from a machine. Although we weren't fully aware of it, he was quickly dying from emphysema. He had been staying at our house for the week so that we could watch over him while my mother-in-law underwent a medical procedure.

As I was passing by him on the couch, he reached out to hold my hand. With the small amount of breath that he had, he whispered to me, "Susan, every day I pray that God will take me and give you a healthy child." At this time, children with HIV/AIDS weren't living past ten or twelve years.

"What makes you think that I want more children?" I responded in my most lighthearted manner as I pointed to the children who were running through the room. That was the only way I could answer; I was not ready to acknowledge how seriously close he was to death. He had been the only father I knew, and he was a good one.

In a very short time, my father-in-law had also become a good grandfather to our children. Our contentious argument from before the adoption had never been mentioned again. Once he met the children, he fell in love with them on the spot. He couldn't do physical things with them, but he would do puzzles or silly word games. The children, especially Mihaela, liked to wait on him by bringing him his meals in the living room.

My father-in-law died in January 1995; I was pregnant by March, and Aidan was due on December 2, my father-in-law's birthday, though he entered the world on December 13. We were sure that Bill's dad, Joseph, had sent Aidan Joseph our way. What other way is there to explain why, after twenty-four years of never conceiving a child, I did? For me, there's no other answer.

AFTERWORD

Our family's story is included in a book, *Ordinary Grace*, by Kathleen A. Brehony, whose central theme is questioning why people do good things in life. I assume that people who haven't done the right thing have been studied; this author wanted the other side of the story. The problem was that the author didn't come up with a conclusive enough answer for me. I wanted that answer, and I wanted it clearly spelled out. To contribute to the children of Casa Speranta, to give them a chance at life, and to see them grow and thrive was to experience a miracle. And then bringing four of these beautiful children home with me was more than I could have imagined. Was this gift a once-in-a-lifetime experience? Or was this what some might refer to as a "calling"? Was I being greedy, wanting to know how to get more of this kind of experience? These are the questions. In telling our story, I thought I might find the answers because I had been one of these people. What made other people in Kathleen's book and me not question why they became so involved in helping others that they entered uncharted territory without a compass or map?

Through this writing, I learned a deeper under-standing of the heart's intelligence, to acknowledge the heart's ability to move us further and reach higher than we ever thought possible. I believe that it is our connection to our hearts that leads all of us to do good. It was the fire that ignited three people, Brother Toby, Sister Marti, and Sister Julie, to take on such a monu-mental task of helping Romania's children.

Through the media, other people's hearts were touched. People responded nationwide; some gave up what they were doing, joined Brother Toby, and vol-unteered. In my experience, my heart led me to the unexpected. It gave me the gift of knowing I made a difference. As I wrote to Brother Toby, I thought that these children had something to teach me. From my first days with Tina, the lessons were presented to me. Through Tina, I learned about hope as a new way of being in this world. I no longer see hope as passive, something to be waited for; hope is active and quick-ened by its connection with love. Casa Speranta (the House of Hope) was my schoolroom of hope, the chil-dren being the masters of this art.

From my children, I have continued to learn about my strengths and weaknesses. Our children are brave. They have taught me to be strong as I watched them be pioneers in their battle to live fully with HIV/AIDS. They have helped me heal some of my childhood trauma as they approached theirs. And through them, I came to believe in miracles. I now have four children to love, and be loved by, who were not expected to live into their teens. Plus, the miracle of Aidan, who came to us in my forty-fifth year and after twenty-four years of marriage.

In telling the story, I saw how many times my most meaningful experiences have happened when I allowed myself to know from my heart. Without question, my heart brought me to Bill at a young age. He was to be my life partner; his love has been there to give me the support, encouragement, and security that I needed to live as fully as I could. He is the man who echoed my dream when he said, "We can't adopt just one; we have to go for all five. How would we ever choose?"

He has brought never-ending laughter into my life, which has nurtured my soul. When he and I questioned our love for each other, our hearts were persistent in bringing us back together. Through a new way of knowing, we were moved from a lower-level relationship to a higher understanding of what love is.

My desire for this book is to acknowledge that our heart has an intelligence of its own. To remind us that our mind, with all its knowledge, is not our only way of knowing. The heart is more than a sentimental valentine; when valued, it has a wisdom of its own.

This book came from my heart. When I started it, I didn't know exactly why I wanted to write it, but I did not need to understand. I trusted the feeling that I have come to honor. I knew the why of it would show itself; that is the way of the heart.

ACKNOWLEDGMENTS

I wish to thank many of the people who inspired this book:

- Brother Toby, Sister Marti, and Sister Julie, for showing me the way through your courage and commitment to God's children.

- Dr. Matusa, gentle warrior, your fight for children with AIDS inspired me.

- Dr. Zugravescu, for the sake of the children, changed her mind and made the impossible possible; for this, I am grateful.

- Simona, for your love and support since the beginning.

- Ellyn, for knowing what I needed before I did.

In their desire to help our children, I also wish to acknowledge:

- The Elizabeth Glaser Pediatric AIDS Foundation

- Dr. Whitley-Williams, Chief of the Division of Pediatric Allergy, Immunology, and Infectious Diseases at Rutgers Robert Wood Johnson Medical School

- The Learning Studio/Dorscher family

Thanks, too, to Dr. George Lombardi for your encouragement to share my story, and to Billie Fitzpatrick—synchronicity opened the door to this book; you showed me the way.

The numerous friends and family who have been there for our family over the years is overwhelming. To try to list them by name fills me with a sense of dread that I might forget to thank someone. So it is with immense gratitude that I want to acknowledge all our friends and family who opened their arms and hearts to us. Your love is what it's all about.

Printed in the USA
CPSIA information can be obtained
at www.ICGtesting.com
CBHW081643181223
2730CB00018B/337

9 798218 962432